Praise for *Embracing Communist China: America's Greatest Strategic Failure*

"Fanell and Thayer's *Embracing Communist China* provides a detailed and valuable examination of how the U.S. national security community failed in identifying the national security threat from the People's Republic of China (PRC) over the past forty years. While there was a clear lack of recognition of the growing threat, it is particularly alarming given the very strong indications and warning including affirmative, bellicose statements by the PRC of their intent. Even today the US approach is one of "wishing away" the threat rather than dealing with it head on. The book's findings and first-hand observations are an especially important topic given the current state of PRC threats to the Indo-Pacific region and America. This excellent manuscript goes on to provide practical solutions on how to restore America's national defense vis-a-vis the PRC; solutions that should be adopted with a sense of urgency."
—John Bird, Vice Admiral, US Navy (retired), former commander, US Seventh Fleet

"In the more than two centuries of American foreign policy mistakes, failures, and debacles, one stands out: Washington's post-Cold War inability to understand and defend against the militant People's Republic of China. James E. Fanell and Bradley A. Thayer tell us how the U.S. can avoid the catastrophe that is fast approaching."
—Gordon Chang, American journalist, lawyer, political commentator, and writer

"Successful strategy first understands the past and the present before focusing on the future. In their new book, *Embracing Communist China*, authors Jim Fanell and Brad Thayer provide a fresh perspective on the failure of US past and present relations with China and the Chinese Communist Party. This is a must read for those who truly want to understand the threat our nation faces from the CCP."
—Tony L. Cothron, Rear Admiral, US Navy (retired), former director of Naval Intelligence

"James E. Fanell and Bradley A. Thayer have long warned of the multifaceted threats posed by China to US security. Now in comprehensive fashion, they analyze why, in near suicidal blindness, America ignored these obvious Chinese challenges to our very way of life—documenting how naïveté and condescension about communist agendas, hubris in assuming perpetual and automatic American preeminence, and the financial self-interest of our elites have all combined to ensure China's unwarranted but nonetheless enormous leverage and power over America. This is a rare, much needed, and erudite 11th-hour blueprint of how Americans can wake up, rebuild our defenses, stop fueling Chinese mercantilism, and reassert strategic deterrence to protect our allies and ourselves."
—Victor Davis Hanson, Martin and Illie Anderson Senior Fellow, the Hoover Institution, Stanford University

"America is in World War III. It was begun by the Chinese Communist Party in order to put them in control of the world. With *Embracing Communist China* by James E. Fanell and Bradley A. Thayer, a master work of strategy and politics, they demonstrate how the US defense and political establishment engaged in self-deception about the nature of Communist China and the consequences for our national survival. Anyone looking to understand what steps need to be taken to defend the United States, needs to read this book."

—Brian T. Kennedy, president, the American Strategy Group, chairman, the Committee on the Present Danger: China

"I commend Capt. James E. Fanell and Dr. Bradley A. Thayer for their superlative exposition of the catastrophic failure of all American institutions—intelligence, military, finance, higher education—to protect and defend the United States from infiltration and conquest by the Chinese Communist Party (CCP). It is a sorry tale of elite capture, strategic ineptitude, shameful avarice, told with rigor and precision. The hour is late, as the CCP is waging its "People's War" on the USA, thus I urge every citizen to heed Capt. Fanell and Dr. Thayer's dire warnings and read this book."

—Maura Moynihan, journalist, author, formerly with Radio Free Asia's Tibet bureau

"*Embracing Communist China* is an exceptional and unprecedented analysis of fifty years of appeasement to Communist China. James E. Fanell and Bradley A. Thayer's sharp and insightful assessment of the federal bureaucracy's refusal to confront the PRC matches my own experience from four years in the Trump Administration. Besides documenting this revolting history, these authors provide sound recommendations for returning America's foreign policy to the right course began under President Trump."

—Peter Navarro, former assistant to the President, director of Trade and Manufacturing Policy, and the national Defense Production Act policy coordinator

"James E. Fanell and Bradley A. Thayer's book comes at a critical time in American history as our nation faces its most capable adversary ever: the Chinese Communist Party. As Fanell and Thayer explain, the CCP has captured much of the American elite. Every time the Trump Administration took action to defend the country against China, the White House switchboard would light up with calls from Wall Street titans, Hollywood moguls and Vegas casino magnates demanding a change in policy. Fanell and Thayer are right, we have a problem."

—Robert C. O'Brien, former US National Security Advisor

"*Embracing Communist China* sheds new light on the failures of US policy towards Beijing after the end of the Cold War. The ideas presented in this book are a valuable contribution to the ongoing debate on how the US should confront communist-led China."

—Marco Rubio, US Senator

EMBRACING COMMUNIST CHINA

EMBRACING COMMUNIST CHINA

AMERICA'S GREATEST STRATEGIC FAILURE

JAMES E. FANELL AND BRADLEY A. THAYER

Foreword by Stephen K. Bannon

War Room Books may be purchased in bulk at special discounts for sales
promotion, corporate gifts, fund-raising, or educational purposes. Special
editions can also be created to specifications. For details, contact the Special Sales
Department, Skyhorse Publishing, 307 West 36th Street, 11th Floor, New York,
NY 10018 or info@skyhorsepublishing.com.

War Room Books® is a registered trademarks of Skyhorse Publishing, Inc.®, a
Delaware corporation.

Visit our website at www.skyhorsepublishing.com.
Please follow our publisher Tony Lyons on Instagram @tonylyonsisuncertain

10 9 8 7 6 5 4 3 2 1

Library of Congress Cataloging-in-Publication Data is available on file.

Cover design by David Ter-Avanesyan
Cover photo credit: Shutterstock

Print ISBN: 978-1-64821-059-4
Ebook ISBN: 978-1-64821-060-0

Printed in the United States of America

To my father, for teaching me what real success is all about—obedience to God; and to Admiral Donald "Mac" Showers who patiently passed along his experiences working for Commander Joe Rochefort, who played a significant role in America's victory at the Battle of Midway. All three men lived by the adage that "there is no limit to what can be accomplished so long as you don't care who gets the credit."

J.E.F.

For those insightful, adroit, patriotic, and valiant strategists, scholars, journalists, and practitioners Steve Bannon, Paul Berkowitz, Gordon Chang, June Teufel Dreyer, James Fanell, Rick Fisher, Frank Gaffney, Bill Gertz, Lianchao Han, Brian Kennedy, Charles Kupperman, James Lilley, Andrew Marshall, Andrew May, James Mann, Maura Moynihan, Peter Navarro, Grant Newsham, William Triplett, Arthur Waldron, and Larry Wortzel. Their strategic acumen allowed them to perceive and warn of the danger when the vast majority were willfully blind, deaf, dismissive, naively idealistic, or actively assisting the enemy.

B.A.T.

TABLE OF CONTENTS

LIST OF FIGURES AND TABLE

***

Figure 1
Front page of *The Washington Post*'s May 8, 1994 "Outlook" section article "Inside China's Scary New Military-Industrial Complex" by William C. Triplett, II.

Figure 2
PLA Navy Senior Captain Yang Wei Jun, aboard USS *Kitty Hawk* in port Hong Kong, February 5, 2005.

Figure 3
Chief of Naval Operations (CNO) Adm. John Richardson meets with Adm. Wu Shengli, Commander of the People's Liberation Army Navy (PLAN), at the PLAN headquarters in Beijing, July 18, 2016.

Table 1
Numbers of Certain Types of Chinese and US Ships Since 2005.

ACKNOWLEDGMENTS

Many people assisted us with this book. Steve Bannon encouraged us to advance our arguments and provided an outlet for its publication. We have the good fortune to interview many individuals who are knowledgeable about our topic. For their exceptional comments, we thank Paul Berkowitz, Ólafur Björnsson, Peppi DeBiaso, June Teufel Dreyer, Rick Fisher, Bill Gertz, Lianchao Han, Brian Kennedy, Charles Kupperman, John Lenczowski, Grant Newsham, Kevin Roberts, William Triplett, and Arthur Waldron.

We thank Tony Lyons for his interest in this book from the outset, as well as Jason Katzman, Stephan Zguta, and the production support team at Skyhorse Publishing. We're grateful to Mark Amundsen for his careful copy-editing also greatly appreciate the permission of Thomas Kerr for his gracious permission to use the illustration, Figure 1, from thirty years ago.

Finally, we thank our wives, Cornelia and Eike, and families for allowing us the time to devote to the book.

FOREWORD

BY STEPHEN K. BANNON

The greatest betrayal in history has been that of the American and Chinese people by the American elite in league with the Chinese Communist Party (CCP). Wall Street and pro-Engagement experts in government have funded and supported the CCP for decades. That support kept the CCP in power and empowered their illegitimate and tyrannical rule to continue and sustain the appalling abuses of the Chinese people. That support also gave rise to the greatest external threat the United States has ever faced as, year-after-year, the People's Republic of China's (PRC) military grew stronger, and their threat to America's national security and our allies grew greater and more immediate.

The horrific damage Wall Street and Big Finance did was not limited to the PRC. They supported the grotesque policy of offshoring American manufacturing and jobs to the People's Republic of China (PRC), and so the destruction of the American working and middle classes. Likewise, they facilitated the loss of American intellectual property and manufacturing knowhow to the PRC. In sum, they robbed Americans of the American Way of Life. The CCP's sponsorship of the chemical weapons attack that is fentanyl cost so many Americans their lives, their health, and their wellbeing.

The evil partnership between the PRC, Wall Street, and national security elites used their wealth and influence to corrupt the American political system, including politicians of both parties, to gain political power. While this started in the Clinton administration, it continued in all subsequent ones with the important exception of the Trump presidency. Only President Trump

XVI   EMBRACING COMMUNIST CHINA

recognized the true nature of the CCP and the existential threat it posed to the American people.

They employed their lucre to pervert and contaminate America's educational system and universities, legacy and social media, law firms and tech centers like Silicon Valley, publishing houses, philanthropic foundations, NGOs, think tanks, and governmental institutions, state, local, and territorial governments, and the Chamber of Commerce. In fact, the rot is so deep that it is far easier to make a list of those groups not corrupted by CCP influence than those that were.

James Fanell and Bradley Thayer have taken the first step toward providing an accounting of this betrayal as well as how to save the United States from this perilous situation. *Embracing Communist China: America's Greatest Strategic Failure* is the best analysis of how the United States made the fundamental mistake of aiding its enemy. The end of the Cold War was the best chance to get rid of the CCP. The CCP leadership knew this. They were determined not to share the fate of the Soviet Union. They realized they could buy influence with Wall Street, Big Finance, and politicians, and by making them partners, they would support the CCP's rule, come what may. It was Satanic genius. But it required Americans on Wall Street, Big Finance, and in government to place their greed before their country. They did. Now all Americans incur the costs.

Second, this book is exceptional because it shows the failure of US presidents except Trump, US intelligence community, and military to act against the CCP. Year after year they did nothing while the threat grew in front of their noses. US military power vis-à-vis the People's Liberation Army (PLA) was purposefully allowed to degrade to the point that now the services are pressed to confront this threat with insufficient forces in both size and capability; this is most especially true of the US Navy. Likewise, US nuclear weapons capabilities atrophied, while the PRC grew at a breathtaking pace. They preferred illusion and mythology to understanding power politics and Communist ideology. Those are the tools needed to grasp the harsh reality of the CCP. To this day, it remains difficult to get the US national security community to see the threat and act against it. The unhindered rise of the PRC to pose an existential threat to America is the greatest failure of the American national security community.

Third, the study provides immediate steps to take to address the threat. What American national security elites must now do is admit that they failed and must throw the rudder of the ship of state hard over—to the principles of power politics vis-à-vis the PRC. Executing this rudder change within the foreign policy community will take years of consistent pressure to reverse—as can already be clearly seen from the sudden resumption of visits to the PRC by senior cabinet level officials from the Biden administration. But the most important step that the US needs to take is to target the CCP directly. They are the center of gravity. With their defeat, their strangle hold on the Chinese people will be broken and the greatness of the Chinese people may come once again to the fore. With their defeat, the American people will have eliminated the greatest threat of the twenty-first century to American safety and security. With their defeat, the exploitation of people and the environment that defines the CCP will be terminated.

Despite its profound mistakes, naïve and gormless leadership, and the grievous and lasting errors of the US national security community, the US will defeat the CCP. The CCP now faces great vulnerabilities, a giant with feet of clay, and can be sent to the dustbin of history if the US will act. Fanell and Thayer have warned us now is the time to defeat its tyranny. Fanell and Thayer have shown key actions of how to do so. What has been absent is the will to defeat the CCP. Now US presidents and Congress must have the will to act. Now is the time to sound the death knell of the Chinese Communist Party.

EXECUTIVE SUMMARY

The book explains why the United States underestimated the threat from the People's Republic of China (PRC) for decades and the lessons and implications of this profound strategic miscalculation. Since the end of the Cold War, the US has made two fundamental and interrelated grand strategic mistakes. First, the failure to perceive the threat from the PRC. Second, the failure to balance against it to defeat the PRC. As a result of these mistakes, the US is at risk of losing its dominant position in global politics. The central question of this book is: how did this happen? How was it possible that the US could achieve victory in the Cold War to the strategic condition today, where it faces a peer enemy?

First, the US failed to perceive the PRC threat due to the dramatic change in the distribution of power in the US's favor due to the collapse of the Soviet Union. This left the US without a peer threat as the PRC was then a minor power. The US entered a long period of what the authors designate "threat deflation," where US dominance and post 9/11 diversion of attention toward the War on Terror, as well as the PRC's masterful political warfare campaign, prevented the US national security community from meeting the peer competitive threat of the PRC and the requirements of high intensity warfare.

The end of the Cold War yielded triumphalism of the "End of History," and thus caused the ideological and strategic disarmament of the US as democracy and free market economics were triumphant. Modernizing states like the PRC were on the path to democratization and free market economics. Consequently, the Department of Defense, the Intelligence Community (IC), and the lack of leadership from successive administrations neglected to sustain a focus on peer competitive threats.

As time passed, military officers were not taught by professional military education and strategists to comprehend great power politics, peer competition, and Communist ideology, and so generations of military officers rose to command without that fundamental understanding. The result was a historical case of threat deflation—where the US consistently underestimated the PRC threat.

Second, finance and avarice trumped strategy. US business interests and financiers consistently and indefatigably sought economic gain from cooperation with the PRC, treating the Chinese people as the source of cheap physical labor for manufacturing, investment, as well as inexpensive intellectual labor, including for research and development. This facilitated the PRC's rise, the sustainment of Most Favored Nation (MFN) trade status, and ultimately admission to the World Trade Organization (WTO). Their influence on the major US political parties and at the highest levels of US politics hindered the US response and promoted the conceit of globalization.

Thus emerged an "engagement school," which asserted that by engaging the PRC, it would become wealthy and in time democratic. In addition, the US welcomed hundreds of thousands of intelligent, serious, and diligent Chinese students to run US and Western scientific labs and numerous academic departments in engineering, and in the life and natural sciences, especially chemistry, computer science, genetics, mathematics, and physics. In essence, the US willingly and enthusiastically taught, trained, and even equipped its mortal enemy—the PRC. Business interests and financiers also funded think tanks, including major national security think tanks and media, which, in turn, contributed to a bias toward the engagement school of thought, and thus the consistent underestimation of the PRC threat.

Third, the US's enemies were great strategists. Led by Deng Xiaoping and the Chinese Communist Party (CCP), the PRC advanced a political warfare strategy to promote threat deflation that was adopted by the US national security establishment. Deng also profited from studying and improving upon Soviet efforts to penetrate US society as well as learning key lessons from the Soviet Union's mistakes in the Cold War.

The PRC successfully caused threat deflation by adopting a complex strategy. They focused on elites in all aspects of US and other Western societies, enriching them and shaping their perception of the PRC and of the CCP, while using the enticement of a growing market to influence their behavior. For a generation, the PRC masked their intentions and framed their expansion as economic rather than strategic, an unalloyed good that would benefit the world.

The book is significant for five reasons. First, the rise of the PRC from minor state to peer competitor was a profound strategic failure for the United States and the greatest failure of the US military and Intelligence Community (IC). The US national security community must understand why this occurred and what must be accomplished to correct it.

Second, the study explains how the PRC executed a political warfare campaign to manipulate US threat perception and reduce the risk of balancing against Beijing by the US. This is necessary to comprehend to avoid its reoccurrence and to understand accurately the CCP's motivations and capabilities as it continues to pursue its stated goal of achieving the Great Rejuvenation of the PRC to become the world's sole superpower.

Third, this analysis corrects the misapprehension and mistaken beliefs regarding the CCP threat, particularly with respect to the inherent aggression of its Communist ideology, which are still present in the US national security community and among financiers, business leaders, academics, scientists, and many others, in the US and allied countries.

Fourth, understanding the causes of this failure provides the opportunity to rebuild the study of strategy within the US national security community to combat peer competitive threats and advance a renaissance of US strategic thought to restore the principles of US national security and forge a modern-day victory plan as their predecessors did in 1941.

Fifth, the study presents the logic of power politics. Its logic defeats the PRC's threat deflation campaign by accurately characterizing the PRC threat across all domains of national power. This allows Americans to have the complete identification of the PRC threat and how to defeat it. Additionally, the logic of the power politics to perceive its permanent national security interests and responsibilities in the Indo-Pacific and across the globe.

The study provides nine implications of the study's arguments to correct these problems, which are organized into three sections: first, power politics and the principles of strategy; second, the PRC's tactics to influence the US elite; and third, how the IC failed.

First, the fundamental importance of power politics for framing threats to US national security and policy responses must be comprehended by national security decision-makers. Understanding power politics permits realistic assumptions about the future of the Sino-American relationship and Washington's relationship with other great powers. The change in the distribution of power to the great favor of Washington had a dramatic effect. The US national security community became vulnerable to threat deflation, weakened its ability to evaluate great power threats, and had a profoundly difficult time adjusting to the new distribution of power with the PRC's rise.

Second, the US must support the education of strategists so that younger generations may possess the knowledge they need in the fight against PRC. Education in the principles of power politics is essential so that strategists have the intellectual firepower to identify what must be accomplished to achieve victory in the fight against the CCP.

Third, understanding of the ideology of Communism and thus why the PRC had the intention to attack and defeat the US is essential for senior civilian and military national security officials. The CCP's ideology explains its motivation to fight the US until the US is defeated. It will not moderate through engagement or compromise, and it will never become democratic. Equally, understanding the CCP's ideology explains why the CCP is illegitimate and possesses profound weaknesses.

Fourth, the absence of presidential leadership in the post-Cold War period has hindered the ability of national security decision-makers to formulate a strategy to defeat the CCP threat. The interests of US business and Wall Street, among others, which sought engagement with the PRC predominated. In addition, the horrific attacks on 9/11 and its consequences, most importantly the Iraq War, also had a profoundly adverse impact. Many of the problems identified in this study could have been resolved if there were adequate presidential leadership.

Fifth, the failure of the US intelligence community to identify the PRC as an existential threat greatly weakened the ability of national security decision-makers to identify and act against the threat. The fundamental assumptions regarding the CCP and the PRC's behavior seem to have been informed by the engagement school of thought. Ultimately, the IC was aiding threat deflation, and never seemed to have conducted analyses of the CCP and PRC's strategy and intentions through the lens of power politics.

Sixth, the failure of military leadership to recognize and prepare for the rise of the PRC is not limited to the presidency or IC. The uniformed military leadership must also be held accountable for America's current state of military unpreparedness. Specifically, the failure of the US Navy leaders to recognize the centrality of the maritime domain to the PRC's grand strategy and the concurrent naval modernization efforts by the PLA Navy stands in stark contrast to pro-active performance of prior generations of admirals from World War II through the Cold War with the Soviet Union.

Seventh, the minor war today in Afghanistan or Iraq was always more important than the major war with the PRC later. The necessity of fighting wars against terrorists and insurgents dominated US national security decision-makers in the post-Cold War era. The direct result was the PRC achieving peer competitive status without any effective opposition. This has been especially damaging given the US position in Afghanistan and Iraq has been lost as well.

Eighth, the lack of examination of assumptions had a pernicious impact on US national security following decades of following threat deflation. This included, first, that history was at its end, and great power threats were an artifact of the past, and therefore cooperation with Russia or the PRC was benign from the perspective of US national security. Second, there was a bias that the US possesses the assumption of time to address future problems and existential threats to the US. The third assumption was that the PRC would be positively transformed through the coterie of engagement policies.

Ninth, it was a testament to the success of the Deng's strategy of threat deflation that the PRC's influence was so easily able to penetrate the financial interests of US firms, media, think tanks, and of individuals, including politicians—otherwise known as "elite capture." The problem of elite capture was that far too many US politicians and officials, in addition to businesses, financiers, media, academics, think tanks, foundations, were profiting from the PRC's rise. Thus, these parties had an interest in threat deflation and shaping analyses that favored engagement and cooperative policies.

Regarding the specific measures that the US should undertake, we argue that the US national security community should adopt nine necessary measures. First, American national security elites must now admit that they failed and must throw the rudder of the ship of state hard over—to the principles of power politics vis-à-vis the PRC—if America and all that it stands for is to have any chance of survival against its CCP enemy.

Second, Americans must understand that the existing distribution of power within the US national security community is resistant to withdrawing from the engagement school of thought—their predilection will be to return the rudder of the ship of state to amidships and the course toward engagement with the PRC.

Third, executing this rudder change within the foreign policy community will take years of consistent pressure—as can already be clearly seen from the sudden resumption of visits to the PRC by senior cabinet level officials from the Biden administration.

Fourth, while significant challenges have been identified by this study, there is reason to be optimistic because of America and the great strengths that come from our Declaration, Constitution, and 247 years of history.

Fifth, America's victory over these internal and external forces is only possible if action is taken now. Given the shift in the balance of power toward Beijing and the existence of the CCP's "timeline" for the Great Rejuvenation, it must be understood that action to prevent the final destruction of our nation must be taken immediately.

Sixth, as in the Cold War, the US needs to create a "Team B" dynamic to address the threat. A Team B for the PRC is needed that would bring together individuals from industry, scientists, negotiators, academics, and government service to create "quick fixes" to the immediate problems of the PRC threat.

Seventh, again, as in the Cold War, Soviet doctrine was well studied by the US national security community to discern where the Soviets were investing, what they were developing, and the force structure they were creating and the missions that force structure could support. Today, the US needs to have the same familiarity with the PLA's doctrine to understand their priorities for investment, research, and force structure development, and the missions and options that force structure would support.

Eighth, the US needs to support nuclear proliferation in the case of Japan, South Korea, and Taiwan, to complicate the PRC's strategic calculus. Nuclear proliferation introduces considerable risks, notably the incentive of the PRC to arrest it, including by military action, before a state becomes nuclear. But the benefits for the US as well as for these states is that each would have a strong deterrent.

Ninth, the US needs to take bold action to target the CCP directly. This requires a multifaceted approach that will include the rollback the PRC's gains in the South China Sea, and the defeat of the PRC in its attempted coercion of the Philippines at Second Thomas Shoal. The US and its allies will have to evict the PRC from facilities in other countries like Djibouti and Ream, Cambodia. Those are important and necessary measures to place Beijing on the strategic backfoot. But the center of gravity that the US must attack is the CCP itself to ensure that the CCP, the Chinese people, and all global audiences know that it is illegitimate, and that the US, working with the Chinese people and allies, is working to evict it from power.

CHAPTER ONE

THE ROOTS OF THE PROBLEM

———

The People's Republic of China (PRC) rose from being a Third World state to being a peer competitor to the US in about thirty years. Remarkably, the US did not recognize this strategic trendline and did not adopt a policy to stop the PRC's rise. Now it faces a Herculean task of defeating this existentially dangerous competitor. The US has made two fundamental and related grand strategic mistakes. First, it did not identify the threat for decades. Second, the US has neglected to act to defeat it. Post-Cold War strategists squandered the gains of previous generations who won World War II, the Cold War, and thus caused the "Pax Americana"—the period of stability in international politics made possible by dominant US power. All they had to do was to keep it. But they did not. With the PRC's rise, they betrayed their predecessors and the American people. As a result, the US again faces a formidable peer.

Accordingly, the US is now in a new Cold War. The Sino-American security competition is the great struggle of the twenty-first century and promises to resolve the dispositive question of the age—whether the world be free and protected by the US or fall into a totalitarian abyss as sought by the PRC. This question will impact US national security, those of its allies, the continuation of US-led liberal order, and of the definitive political principles in international politics.

Uniquely in international politics and in the history of the United States, this perilous situation need not have happened. Over decades, the US had ample time to prevent the PRC's rise and to retard its growth, even to support the overthrow of the CCP, but it did not. Those strategic choices must be explained—why did the US assist, not prevent, the rise of its peer challenger? It was a historically unique case of what we term threat deflation and, as a result, the US underestimated the threat, year after year. This threat deflation was the cause of the CCP's rise without US balancing against it, and so is directly responsible for the gravest strategic mistake ever made by the US, one which today imperils the US homeland, economic prosperity, and national security.

The proclivity of states is to identify threats accurately or more frequently to overestimate them. Thus, threat deflation is rare and is understudied. The result is that too few strategists posed the question of the PRC's rise and its consequences for the US. Further, threat deflation inhibited the creation of a defined school of thought regarding the PRC's rise as there are in other major strategic issues, for example, over US grand strategy or nuclear deterrence. Faced with the PRC threat, too few national security strategists wanted to explain how the US arrived at this position and why, decade after decade, America continued to support the PRC's growth or to acknowledge that the US has arrived at a position where the PRC is able to threaten US national security interests globally. Threat deflation also blinded the national security community to the greatest challenge to the US military's ability to defend the country's national interests in a highly competitive security competition since the Soviet Union.

This failing implicates the US national security community. The PRC's rise without balancing from the US is an international political coup that would rival the achievements of Bismarck, Metternich, Talleyrand, or other great statesmen in history. This is a multi-decade failing of the US strategic community and defines the woeful neglect of the PRC threat by presidential administrations, the US intelligence community (IC), centers of professional military education, national security think tanks, and Sinologists. It is also the result of external events like 9/11 and then the Iraq War, which resulted in a decades-long involvement in southwest Asia to which the services adapted, as did the focus of US strategic thought.

Now the US faces a situation where the PRC has risen to the point where Beijing's aggression against Taiwan and other US interests in the Indo-Pacific are anticipated in this "Decade of Concern" (2020–2030).[1] New PRC kinetic military capabilities, like supersonic and hypersonic weapons, are now targeting US carrier strike groups, which have insufficient hypersonic defensive capabilities. The strategic terrain has been altered dramatically since the days of unrivaled US military power, where US capabilities provided overwhelming deterrence and warfighting capabilities against its foes. The US now operates in an environment where the relative distribution of power has shifted against the United States. It is likely to be in this environment—a new Cold War—until it either defeats the PRC or is defeated by it.

The Central Arguments and Outline

The study explains why the United States underestimated the threat from the PRC for decades and the lessons and implications of this profound strategic miscalculation. It advances three major arguments that account for the US failure and provides nine implications to correct the greatest strategic mistake made by the US. Finally, it presents nine recommendations about what the US needs to do now to assist the defeat of the CCP.

First, the US national security community failed. The US did not perceive the PRC threat due to the dramatic change in the relative distribution of power in the US's favor due to the collapse of the Soviet Union. This left the US without a peer threat as the PRC was a minor power. The US national security entered a period of structural threat deflation, where US dominance and minor wars prevented the US national security community from meeting the peer competitive threat of China and the requirements of high-intensity warfare. The end of the Cold War yielded the triumphalism of the "End of History," and thus caused the ideological and strategic disarmament of the US where democracy and free market economics where triumphant. The firm belief was that modernizing states, including the PRC, were on the path to democratization and free market economics. The elite consensus was that the future would be globalization, while power politics in great power relations was an artifact of the past—a dangerous and unhealthy aspect of great power behavior that they needed and now could move beyond.

Consequently, the major national security actors including the Department of Defense and the IC with the lack of leadership from successive administrations, failed to sustain a focus on peer competitive threats. As time passed, military officers were not taught by professional military education and strategists to comprehend power politics as the organizing principle of great power politics and peer competition. Nor were they taught the salient facts about Communist ideology—particularly its inherent aggression toward the US and its employment of political warfare to shape Western perceptions of the PRC. Consequently, generations of military officers rose to command without that understanding. The result was a historical case of threat deflation—for decades, the US consistently underestimated the PRC threat.

Second, avarice and finance trumped strategy. US business interests and financiers consistently and indefatigably sought economic cooperation with the PRC, treating the Chinese people as the source of cheap physical labor for manufacturing, investment, as well as inexpensive intellectual labor, including for research and development. This facilitated the PRC's rise through the sustainment of Most Favored Nation (MFN) trade status and its admission to the World Trade Organization (WTO). By engaging the PRC, the engagement school, hereafter referred to as the pro-CCP school, asserted, it would become wealthy and in time democratic. In addition, the US welcomed hundreds of thousands of intelligent, serious, and diligent Chinese students to run US and Western scientific labs and numerous academic departments in computer science and engineering, and in the life and natural sciences, especially chemistry, computer science, genetics, mathematics, and physics. In essence, the US willingly and enthusiastically taught and trained its enemy. Business interests and financiers also funded think tanks, including major national security think tanks, media, and universities, which, in turn, contributed to a strong bias toward the pro-CCP school, and thus the consistent underestimation of the PRC threat.

Third, the enemy of the US was an exceptional strategist. The PRC advanced a political warfare strategy to promote threat deflation under Deng Xiaoping. Deng profited from studying and improving upon Soviet efforts to penetrate US society as well as learning key lessons from the Soviet Union's mistakes in the Cold War. The PRC successfully caused threat deflation by adopting a complex strategy. They focused on elites in all aspects of US and other Western societies, enriching them and shaping their perception of the PRC and of the CCP, while using the enticement of a growing market and lucre for their firms, organizations, interests, and for themselves, to influence their behavior.

In essence, Deng employed Adam Smith's "invisible hand" to get US industries and Wall Street to do his work for him. Their self-interest and greed made the PRC the power it is today and secured the CCP's odious rule when it might have been overthrown. Deng made the US Chamber of Commerce, US industry, US investors, and Wall Street, and even the US government partners with the PRC, and all benefited handsomely. For a generation, the PRC masked their intentions and framed their expansion as economic rather than strategic, and an unalloyed good that would benefit the world. It was a masterful political warfare campaign.

Regrettably for US national security, for most of the post-Cold War period, US policymakers—led in part by the State Department—supported the rise of the PRC. Their belief was that a more prosperous PRC would become increasingly democratic, and its integration into the liberal international order would produce a stable and increasingly wealthy PRC. Consequently, the PRC would be supportive of US national security interests and the liberal international order.

In only the last few years, there is a new consensus within the executive branch and Congress supporting increasing confrontation with the PRC.[2] That consensus has been oriented around the central policy goal of confronting China to deter its aggression. It must be said that it is far from clear that this consensus will hold and not be reversed.

Regrettably, there is not yet a consensus regarding how to do so. Approaches are varied, particularly concerning whether the US should seek the overthrow of the CCP. Of course, the defeat of the CCP would be a positive step from the perspective of this study. It would result in orders of magnitude improvements in the Sino-American relationship and advance US national security interests in the Indo-Pacific and globally.

We advance our arguments in the following chapters. Chapter Two introduces the overview of the concept of threat deflation, the logic of power politics, and its application during the Cold War. During the Cold War, power politics' logic explains cooperation with the PRC. Once the Soviet Union was eliminated as a rival, the distribution of power's grip on the minds of US strategists weakened. After the Cold War, its hold was replaced by "End of History" reasoning—that is, the US in the Cold War was the triumph of political liberalism and capitalism, which all states will adopt in time. As a result, US business interests drove engagement with the PRC, facilitated by Deng's political warfare strategy that was adopted by the State Departments and the pro-CCP school.

Unfortunately, 9/11 and its aftermath, most notably the Iraq War, provided the PRC more time to expand without an effective US response. The PRC's power was now formidable, if not clearly a peer of the US, and thus the cost of a US response was considerable. Indeed, it was too great for the Obama administration, as the 2012 Scarborough Shoal incident between the PRC and the Philippines revealed.

Chapter Three provides nine implications of the arguments for the US national security community and the American people that are relevant to the present Sino-American Cold War. These are organized in three categories. First, those relevant to power politics and the principles of strategy. Second, analysis is provided of what the US IC and military did that contributed to failure. Third, what the PRC accomplished to successfully threat deflate is considered.

First, the fundamental importance of power politics concepts for framing threats to US national security and policy responses must be comprehended by senior civilian and military national security decision-makers. Understanding the power politics permits realistic assumptions about the future of the Sino-American relationship and Washington's relationship with other great powers. The change in the distribution of power to the great favor of Washington had a dramatic effect. The US national security community became vulnerable to threat deflation, which weakened its ability to evaluate great power threats and see clearly the changing correlation of forces, and thus the need to adjust US policies to prevent or retard the PRC's rise.

Second, the US national security community must support the education of strategists so that younger generations may possess the knowledge they need in the fight against the PRC. Education in the principles of power politics is essential so that strategists have the intellectual firepower to identify what must be accomplished to achieve victory in the fight against the CCP.

Third, understanding of the ideology of Communism and thus why the PRC had the intention to attack and defeat the US is essential for senior civilian and military US national security officials. The CCP's ideology explains its motivation to fight the US until the US is defeated. It will not moderate through engagement or compromise, and it will never become democratic—because these principles are anathema to the very essence of Chinese Communist ideology. Equally, understanding the CCP's ideology explains why the CCP is illegitimate and possesses profound weaknesses.

Fourth, the absence of presidential leadership to heed the lessons of power politics and strategy in the post-Cold War period has hindered the ability of national security decision-makers to formulate a strategy to defeat the CCP threat. The interests of US business and Wall Street, among others, which furthered engagement with the PRC predominated, as did 9/11 and its aftermath. Many of the problems identified in this study could have been resolved if there were adequate presidential leadership in the decades after the Soviet Union's demise.

Regrettably, there is also a second broad category of problems—those of the IC and the US military who, in their institutional responses missed the PRC threat year after year, and too frequently worked with the PRC to assist it. The forms of assistance took many forms, including helpfully answering the questions of PLA officers as they toured US vessels, including nuclear aircraft carriers and submarines. In this category, some the failings were deeper, such as not examining assumptions, and the dominant concern of the small wars of Afghanistan and Iraq over the big war of the PRC.

Fifth, the failure of the US intelligence community to identify the PRC as an existential threat greatly weakened the ability of national security decision-makers to identify and act against the threat. The fundamental assumptions regarding the CCP and the PRC's behavior seem to have been informed by the pro-CCP school of thought. Ultimately, the IC was aiding threat deflation, and never seem to have conducted analyses of the CCP and PRC's strategy and intentions through the lens of power politics.

Sixth, the failure of military leadership to recognize and prepare for the rise of the PRC are not limited to the presidency or IC. The uniformed military leadership must also be held accountable for America's current state of military unpreparedness. Specifically, the failure of the US Navy leaders to recognize the centrality of the maritime domain to the PRC's grand strategy and the concurrent naval modernization efforts by the PLA Navy stands in stark contrast to pro-active performance of prior generations of admirals from World War II through the Cold War with the Soviet Union.

Seventh, the minor wars in Afghanistan or Iraq were always promoted as being more important than the major war with the PRC later. The necessity of fighting wars against terrorists and insurgents heavily dominated US national security decision-makers from as early as Operation Desert Storm in 1991 through the ignoble retreat from Kabul in 2021. The result was that the peer competitive threat of the PRC grew without effective deterrence from the US, which has been doubly damaging as the US positions in Afghanistan and Iraq have been lost as well.

Eighth, the lack of examination of assumptions was pernicious in the decades of threat deflation. This included, first, that history was at its end, and great power threats were an artifact of the past and therefore cooperation with Russia or the PRC was benign from the perspective of US national security. Second, there was a bias that the US possesses the time to address future problems and existential threats to the US. The third assumption was that the PRC would be positively transformed through an endless coterie of engagement policies.

Finally, there is a third category of troubles—those caused by the enemy. It is often said that the enemy gets a vote, and it always does. But with the PRC, it was more like the enemy was not just casting a vote, but choosing the candidates, counting the votes via voting machines—which might have been literally as well as figuratively the case—and tallying the vote. The PRC was expert at manipulating US business interests and Wall Street to do its biding.

This yields the identification of our ninth failing. It was a testament to the success of the Deng's strategy of threat deflation that the PRC's influence was able to penetrate the financial interests of US firms, media, think tanks, universities, and of many in the elite, including politicians at the federal, state, local, and territorial levels of US government. The problem of elite capture, where far too many US politicians and officials, in addition to business, financiers, media, academics, think tanks, and foundations, were profiting from the PRC's rise. Thus, these parties had a vested interest in threat deflation and shaping analyses that favored engagement and cooperative policies. Deng was a student of the free market, and as we have asserted, while it certainly seems unlikely that he read the great Scottish political economist, he did understand Smith's famous argument regarding the "invisible hand," that self-interested concern for profits will shape behavior. Simply put, Deng was a strategic genius. He made US industry, Wall Street, capital markets, media, think tanks, and even the US government partners in the success of the CCP. That was simply brilliant, if greatly unfortunate for the American people and US national security interests.

Chapter Four presents our analysis of the nine measures that the US should accomplish at this time to defeat the CCP. First, what American national security elites must now do is admit that they failed and must throw the rudder of the ship of state hard over—to the principles of power politics vis-à-vis the PRC—if America and all it stands for is to have any chance of survival against its CCP enemy.

Second, Americans must understand that the existing distribution of power within the US national security community is resistant to withdrawing from the pro-CCP school—their predilection will be to return the rudder of the ship of state to amidships and the course toward engagement with the PRC.

Third, executing this rudder change within the foreign policy community will take years—as can already be clearly seen from the sudden resumption of visits to the PRC by senior cabinet level officials from the Biden administration.

Fourth, while significant challenges have been identified by this study, there is reason to be optimistic because of America and the great strengths that come from our Declaration, Constitution, and our 247 years of history.

Fifth, America's victory over these internal and external forces is only possible if action is taken now. Given the shift in the balance of power toward Beijing and the existence of the CCP's "timeline" for the Great Rejuvenation, it must be understood that action to prevent the final destruction of the nation must be taken immediately.

Sixth, as in the Cold War, the US needs to create a "Team B" dynamic to address the threat. A Team B for the PRC is needed that would bring together individuals from industry, scientists, negotiators, academics, and government service to create "quick fixes" to the immediate problems of the PRC threat.

Seventh, again as in the Cold War, Soviet doctrine was well studied by the US national security community to discern where the Soviets were investing, what they were developing, and the force structure they were creating and the missions that force structure could support. Today, the US needs to have the same familiarity with the PLA's doctrine to understand their priorities for investment, research, and force structure development, and the missions and options that force structure would support.

Eighth, the US needs to support nuclear proliferation in the case of Japan, South Korea, and Taiwan, to complicate the PRC's strategic calculus. Nuclear proliferation introduces considerable risks, notably the incentive of the PRC to arrest it, including by military action, before a state becomes nuclear. But the benefits for the US as well as for these states is that each would have a strong deterrent.

Ninth, the US needs to take bold action to target the CCP directly. This requires a multifaceted approach that will include the rollback the PRC's gains in the South China Sea, and the defeat of the PRC in its attempted coercion of the Philippines at Second Thomas Shoal. The US and its allies will have to evict the PRC from facilities in other countries like Djibouti and Ream, Cambodia. Those are important and necessary measures to place Beijing on the strategic backfoot. However, the center of gravity that the US must attack is the CCP itself to ensure that the CCP, the Chinese people, and all global audiences know that it is illegitimate and that the US, working with the Chinese people and allies, is working to evict it from power with its allies among the Chinese people, its allies, and people of goodwill around the world.

The Significance of the Study

The study is significant for five reasons. First, the rise of the PRC from minor state to peer competitor was a profound strategic failure for the United States and the greatest failure of the US IC. US national security decision-makers and the American people must understand why this occurred over several presidential administrations and what must be accomplished to correct it.

Second, the book explains how the PRC executed a political warfare campaign to manipulate US threat perception and reduce the risk of balancing against Beijing by the US. This is necessary to comprehend in order to avoid its reoccurrence and to understand accurately the CCP's motivations and capabilities. The PRC adopted the political warfare strategy of threat deflation to minimize its growth and the risk this posed to US national security. Accurately perceiving the threat is the first step to meeting the challenges posed by the enemy.

Third, this analysis corrects the misapprehension and mistaken beliefs regarding the CCP threat, particularly with respect to the inherent aggression of its Communist ideology, which are still present among US partners, including among businesses, academics, scientists, and others in the US, allied countries, as well as allied militaries. The flaws of these perceptions must be studied to grasp how the US adopted strategically disastrous policies and threat deflated.

Fourth, understanding the causes of this failure provides the opportunity to rebuild the study of strategy within the national security community to combat peer competitive threats and advance a renaissance of US strategic thought. As strategic thought concerning great power rivals had atrophied in the wake of the Soviet Union's fall, the return of a peer rival compels strategists and professional military education to reflect the change. Fundamental strategic questions concerning the objectives and means employed by the adversary, its center of gravity, its vulnerabilities, and the path to US victory over the PRC, once again must become the focus of US strategists and national security experts.

Fifth, the study presents the logic of power politics. Its logic defeats the PRC's threat deflation campaign by accurately characterizing the PRC threat across all domains of national power. This allows Americans to have the complete identification of the PRC threat and how to defeat it. Additionally, it provides the logic of power politics to perceive its permanent national security interests and responsibilities in the Indo-Pacific and across the globe.

US permanent national security interests in the Indo-Pacific are that no country, such as the PRC, or coalition, such as the PRC and Russia, should possess sufficient power to thwart US national security interests. Thus, the foremost US interest is to preserve its position in international politics as the world's dominant state.[3] From that foundation, US interests that must be defended from the PRC threat, are, first, preserve US security; second, the security of its allies; third, for the promotion of its ideology against rivals to ensure that the twenty-first century is defined by freedom and democratic government, and free markets are the dominant values of international politics; and fourth, to deter the PRC's aggression and the PRC's efforts to entice Japan, India, Russia, or other states into an alliance relationship.

Comprehending permanent US strategic interests allows US national security decision-makers to advance a richer menu of policy options to assist the development of a focused conception of US interests in the Indo-Pacific and the application of its power to preserve them. In turn, this assists the American people to understand their interests in the region. It also assists US allies and adversaries to comprehend US national security interests in the region and globally.

Assumptions and Methodology

There are two principal assumptions of the book. First, this study acknowledges that strategic rivalry between China and the United States is escalating and will continue to do so due to the change in the relative distribution of power and the PRC's Communist ideology and grand strategic ambitions. At present, the signs of increased security competition are ubiquitous in the realm of ideas as well as in diplomacy, economics and trade, intelligence collection, and in power projection. In particular, the development of the PRC's diplomatic, military, and economic might has provided Beijing with the ability to exert a major influence on the development of events in international politics for the first time since the early nineteenth century. This will continue despite the decline in the PRC's economic growth because the PRC now has sufficient capabilities to sustain the competition with the US.

Second, the study assumes that threat deflation may be reversed through the right policy choices and strategies to defeat the PRC's political warfare campaign and its actual as well as *de facto* agents of influence in the US and allied states. This requires that US strategic interests as during the Cold War are able to supplant the interests of finance and business, of Silicon Valley, and in academe, media, foundations, and among elected representatives at the federal, state, local, territorial, and tribal levels to place the security of the country before the interests of firms or investment houses. This is needed so that danger from the PRC may be accurately identified and reversed while there remains time to defeat the PRC.

The methodology of the book is a focused, qualitative advancement of its central arguments. Specifically, the study's methodology is analytic and based on the presentation of why the US threat deflated based upon the historical record and interviews with academics and former military officers and officials concerning the actions of the United States in the aftermath of the Cold War and Deng's "hide and bide" political warfare strategy which was advanced in the early 1990s. Chapter Two contains the presentation of the conceptual logic of the study and the historical foundation.

From this foundation, Chapter Three provides a structured, focused analysis of the major implications for the US national security community and the American people based on the arguments developed using interviews, and historical and analytical methodology. In Chapter Four, the study provides insight into measures that the US should take to accurately identify the PRC threat and to defeat it. Thus, the intent of the analytical arguments of the study are to provide the foundation for the principal implications for the United States.

CHAPTER TWO

THE CAUSES OF THREAT DEFLATION AND ITS CONSEQUENCES

ANALYSIS OF THE CHANGE IN THE DISTRIBUTION OF POWER, THE "END OF HISTORY," AND DENG'S POLITICAL WARFARE STRATEGY

"The strong do what they can, the weak suffer what they must."
—The Melian Dialogue, Thucydides,
History of the Peloponnesian War (5.89–5.90)[1]

What Thucydides wrote in the classic Melian Dialogue of his great work is mostly true. The strong do what they will and the weak have to endure it. Unless the weak are led by a brilliant strategist like the PRC's leader Deng. He knew that the PRC was weak and vulnerable, but far from enduring what he must, he found a way to manipulate the strong through a brilliant political warfare strategy of threat deflating and making the elite in the strong a partner of the PRC's growth. "To get rich is glorious," Deng said. The assumption was that he was referring to China and an embrace of capitalist methods. But there was the hidden meaning, to get rich in China, yes, but also for the elites in the West, it was a glorious way to secure first the PRC's survival, and later, the

15

PRC's dominance. Deng is never mentioned in the pantheon of strategists, but he should be. Deng perceived how he could use his enemy's greed against him. He made his enemy a partner in the CCP's and PRC's success, and his enemy fell for it hook, line, and sinker. Deng and his successors must thank their lucky stars they had an enemy who was so foolish and naïve, so ignorant of power politics and strategy, so callous to human suffering of the Chinese people and also of Americans, who could be bought so cheaply, and who would trade their birthrights—the stable society, country, and world that their fathers and grand-fathers had created and bequeathed—for pennies for a few people at the top.

This chapter provides the foundational argument of the study. It addresses six major topics. First, the chapter introduces the concept of threat deflation. Second, the analysis explains power politics and its relationship to stability in international politics. How power is distributed—that is, how many great powers there are—explains the frequency of great power war. It also explains what great powers should do. At root, they should maximize their power to maximize their security, which means being acutely sensitive to their relative power and doing what they can not to aid the growth of their rival's rela-tive power, for instance, through trade and economic cooperation. Third, it applies the logic of power politics to illuminate US national security policy toward the PRC through the Cold War. Fourth, it elucidates the "End of History" moment and its negative impact upon US national security strategy. Fifth, the chapter analyzes post-Cold War policy toward the PRC, burgeoning economic ties between the US and the PRC, and the role of 9/11 and the costs of the Iraq War. Sixth, it explains Deng's political warfare strategy to enlist US businesses and financiers' support for the PRC's rapid economic and military growth. This chapter serves as the foundation for the analysis in the next chapter.

Threat Deflation

Threat deflation is a rare condition for states as they have a tendency to accu-rately identify and assess threats or to overestimate them. Threat deflation is the consistent underestimation of the threat one state poses to another. It is an intentional strategy usually employed by the weaker power to avoid balancing or attack against it. The strategy is to depress the victim's perception of the threat to gain time for it. In time, if threat deflation is successful, the threat is likely to become so significant that it cannot be misperceived by the victim, but time will have been provided. Threat deflation is accomplished principally by deception. It is successful when the victim state accepts the deflation due to a failure of its intelligence community and/or successful deception due to political idealism, individual ignorance, the discounting by senior decision-makers of the enemy's growth, or a willingness to be deceived because individuals tasked with national security responsibilities have a financial interest in the enemy's rise.

In each instance, threat deception needs only one party to engage in the behavior to have a chance of success. If the elite in the victim state are equally engaged in threat deflation, then it is supremely successful and likely to endure until the conceit is ended by the threat—as it seeks to inherit what it perceives to be its rightful position in global politics—or by the victim as the growth of the threat is increasingly impossible to ignore.

Historically, threat deflation is an atypical trait in international politics. However, it is not an unprecedented activity. For instance, Germany being at the center of great power politics in Europe for two centuries, it is not surprising it adopted threat deflation with relative frequency. First, Prussian and later German Chancellor Otto von Bismarck did this during the wars of German unification with Denmark in 1864, Austria in 1866, and France in 1870–1871. Bismarck sought to signal other European great powers, particularly in the Franco-Prussian War, that his objectives were limited to the immediate war, as he feared the reactions of other great powers.[2] This was acute after 1871, where he wrote of the "bad feeling which has been called out through our growth to the position of real great power."[3] Indeed, the leader of the British Conservative Party, Benjamin Disraeli, wrote that the Franco-Prussian war changed the distribution of power in Europe: "You have a new world, new influences at work, new and unknown dangers with which to cope . . . .The balance of power has been entirely destroyed."[4] Bismarck's penchant for threat deflation also led him to keep the details of 1882 Triple Alliance with Austria-Hungary and Italy and of the 1887 Reassurance Treaty with Russia from the other great powers.

Second, Germany threat deflated with its secret rearmament with the Soviet Union at Rapallo in 1922. The use of Soviet territory for military exercises was instrumental for the development of mobile armored warfare that would defeat France in 1940 but failed outside of Moscow in December 1941.

Third, Nazi Germany also threat deflated with its rearmament and conscription decisions in 1935, both of which were violations of the Versailles Treaty, to the invasion of the rump-Czechoslovakia on March 15, 1939, that is, Bohemia and Moravia, while Slovakia entered a protectorship under Jozef Tiso. A week later, on March 23, 1939, Germany invaded Memel (now Klaipeda, Lithuania). The invasion of the rump-Czechoslovakia (Czechoslovakia absent the Sudetenland), revealed unambiguously the threat of German expansion beyond Germany territories ceded to other states by the Versailles Treaty. These acts resulted in Great Britain's and France's extended deterrent to Poland. Sadly, the deterrent failed. Germany invaded Poland on September 1, 1939, resulting in London's and Paris's declaration of war against Germany two days later.

China threat deflated as well. The Qing Dynasty contemptuously and grossly underestimated the power of Great Britain before the First Opium War (1839–1842) smashed Qing power and commenced the "Century of Humiliation" for China from the First Opium War until 1949, as the CCP perpetually reminds the Chinese people.

While Nazi Germany's effort miscarried once Hitler decided to show his hand as a hyperaggressive leader, the PRC's successful threat deflation is the archetype. The PRC was able to rise as a formidable military, economic, and diplomatic force, pressure neighboring states, and build multilateral institutions, without provoking a balancing coalition against it.

But Germany's, the Qing's, or the PRC's successful cases of threat deflation demonstrate how uncommon effectual cases are. There are many attempted but unsuccessful efforts at threat deflation throughout history, including Bolshevik attempts to minimize their threat as Soviet leader Joseph Stalin built "socialism in one country" and Soviet efforts to do the same during the détente period of the Nixon, Ford, and Carter administrations. Soviet efforts resonated with leftwing political parties in the West and heavily influenced decision-makers during those administrations, but were never without serious and sustained opposition from the Joint Chiefs of Staff, Senators, and Congressmen, the American people, and from allies. In essence, threat deflation is a way to defeat the logic of power politics by minimizing or eliminating the enemy's perception of the threat. It does not usually work. Unfortunately, it did for the PRC.

Power Politics

Power politics and the concern over the distribution of power are defining historical features of international politics dating to the ancient Greeks in the West and the Han Dynasty (202 BC–AD 220) in China. The logic of power politics is that great powers are determined by the correlation of forces and the distribution of power in the international system. That is, how much power they have and how much their rivals possess. Thus, relative power is key—how much power a great power possesses in relation to its rivals—rather than absolute power—how much power it possesses. Each great power is threatened by the other precisely because it has the power to be such a threat.

To provide security for itself, the great power builds its military power to advance and protect its interests. As its own military power is not likely to be sufficient to meet the threats it faces, it must also enlist allies who share the same opponents and so have a mutual interest. Therefore, balancing against the enemy may be internal, generating a state's own military power to meet any threat posed. Or, as is more common in diplomatic history, balancing may also be external, relying on allies to help meet the risks and dangers of international politics because insufficient internal power is able to meet all the threats faced by the state.[5] The consequence of arming and forging alliances is that military power among the great powers will likely be equal. Fundamentally, each will perceive the other as its principal threat, but their balancing should preserve stability, the absence of major war.

In the traditional European balance of power of the eighteenth and nineteenth centuries, the great powers—Austria, France, Great Britain, Prussia, and Russia—were able to balance against their threats so long as each was allied with at least one other great power. Ideally, each great power sought to be among the three great powers aligned against the two, but even allied with only one other great power, sufficient power could be mobilized to balance, however roughly, the three. The result was periods of stability—the absence of great power war—in Europe. Stability was not peace, as minor wars occurred, but the great powers did not fight. Of course, this balance occasionally failed, and resulted in the great power conflicts of European history, such as the French Revolutionary and Napoleonic wars, or World War I. It was at times lopsided as in the Seven Years War when Frederick the Great of Prussia stood against the European powers—and quite successfully as it turned out, given the distribution of power against Prussia—with only Great Britain as an ally.

As European history reveals, allies are necessary, if at times not an unalloyed blessing. In general, the more power a great power possesses, it is a better and more worthy ally. Allies are thus more willing to support the hegemon, the dominant great power of an era, as it requires. The plethora of US allies captures this. The fact that over 80 states have an alliance relationship with the United States is an indication of each of these factors in addition to the fact that states want to use US military power to advance their aims. Having allies also is the closest to a vote of confidence in world politics.

Conversely, the loss of allies is the closest to a vote of no confidence and can lead to a rapid change in the distribution of power. Allies back away from supporting a great power or hegemon because its status is increasingly uncertain, and there is little desire to be on the wrong side of the rising, soon to be dominant, competitor. Indeed, there is the whiff of this today in the Sino-American rivalry. It makes sense for regional allies to hedge their bets and begin increasing their own military capabilities or enter an overt or tacit alliance relationship with the rising great powers or hegemon.

The logic of power politics is that great powers should balance against the aggregate capabilities of other great powers, according to the theorist of international politics Kenneth Waltz—or, more precisely, they should balance against the threat posed by other states, as Waltz's student Stephen Walt argues.[6] Traditionally, power politics emphasizes balancing against the power of other states, that is, capabilities rather than threat. By power, the focus is on the size and health of the economy and military might, although a host of factors including geography, natural resources, and military effectiveness can affect the calculus of power. Power politics advocates agree with Mao Zedong's famous observation that "political power grows out of the barrel of a gun."

While power politics does not submit that the balancing dynamic it depicts inevitably results in war, it does view the use of force as one of the options always available to great power should they conclude that diplomacy alone is ineffective or there is an opportunity to gain at another's expense. Power politics only suggests that the resort to force is possible, not inevitable, and it does not explain which great power will initiate the conflict.

Consequently, power politics does not determine which great power will resort to force. For international relations theorists, the decisive factor determining whether balancing will be peacefully conducted or result in war is the number of great powers in the international system, that is, whether there are two equal great powers, a condition known as bipolarity, or three or more roughly matched great powers, known as multipolarity.

Classical theorists of power politics like George Kennan, Hans Morgenthau, or Nicolas Spykman drew their insights from European politics during the classic age of diplomacy before the French Revolution and again after the defeat of Napoleon in 1815 to the start of World War I. They argued that multipolarity was more stable—there was less likelihood of great power war because each great power had respected spheres of influence and would be conservative in foreign policy, lest one or more of their allies abandoned them as a reckless great power.

The implication of this is that were the world to return to multipolarity with the United States, China, and India equally powerful, at least in an aggregate sense, great power conflict need not occur, and the Sino-American rivalry might be tempered by the weight of India's power, which should alter the balance of power well to the side of the US. Indeed, it is to the great benefit of the United States if India were aligned with it against China, as their combined might could check China's ambitions—a classic two-against-one that might be sufficient to deter China's aggression.[7]

In contrast, drawing on the experience of the Cold War, Waltz argued that bipolarity—two superpowers—was more stable.[8] The reasons the Cold War stayed cold according to Waltz is because bipolarity meant each superpower had only one adversary. Having only one enemy contributed to stability for three reasons. First, the only state that had the power to seriously challenge the United States was the Soviet Union and the reverse. Moreover, the only country that could destroy the United States was the Soviet Union, and, again, the reverse was true.

Second, because of the prodigious power of the two poles—each was not a great power but a superpower—they did not require allies to ensure their security. Because of this, the security of the United States did not depend on its allies. Indeed, its allies needed the United States more than the United States needed them. For example, France could terminate its commitment to the military structure of NATO in 1966 without destroying that alliance or threatening the security of the United States. The Soviet Union could lose its great ally the PRC in the Sino-Soviet split without jeopardizing the safety of the Soviet Union. Not depending upon allies freed the US and the USSR from some of the problems of alliances, such as Germany's calculus in the summer of 1914 that it had to back Austria-Hungary fully or risk its own destruction.

The third reason that bipolarity is more stable is that both superpowers get to know the other very well. Both Moscow and Washington studied the other intensively. One example of this was the nascent science of Kremlinology developed by the United States national security community. Another would be the characterization of the United States as the "main adversary" by the KGB. The central focus of both intelligence communities was the other. Although there were intelligence failures for both sides, the fundamental consequence of this reciprocal understanding was that the risk of conflict due to misperception was reduced, as was the risk that a crisis would escalate. Of course, such risks could never entirely be eliminated.

There was concern among power politics theorists that the rise of the PRC would be only one of several challenges to the hegemony of the United States. There were concerns that Russia, a resurgent Japan, and India would emerge as peer competitors. Were that to have happened, theorists of power politics were concerned about the higher likelihood of war for the reasons that Waltz identified. In addition, key political influences that reduced the dangers of multipolarity in Europe after the Cold War—consensus on the lessons from the past fighting of wars, long experience at international diplomacy, and the stability of domestic political orders—were absent in East Asia. Moreover, democracy is not as widespread, there are relatively few institutions, and none with the strength of NATO in Europe, and territorial disputes are numerous.

Today, international politics is more complicated than the Cold War. There is certainly the bipolar Cold War between China and the United States and bipolar tension between China and India. But the world is increasingly and simultaneously multipolar as China, India, and the United States possess far more power than other great powers. For power politics theorists heavily influenced by Waltz's arguments, bipolarity should be a force for stability between China and the US, and between China and India, but multipolarity a source of conflict for the reasons Waltz identified. Accordingly, the risks are far greater than considered by power politics advocates. The dangers of miscalculation are significantly greater because of the boldness of and determination to confront the United States possessed by the PRC's Communist leadership. In sum, viewing the contemporary distribution of power through the lens of power politics results in the expectation of profound danger in the Sino-American relationship, whether the future of international politics is bipolar or multipolar.

As in the past, power politics is a useful instrument to explain this period of international history. Throughout history, the dangers identified by power politics have repeated themselves as great powers have made decisions for war based on efforts to influence the distribution of power in their favor. Empirically, this has led to the successes of Frederick the Great, Louis XIV, Wilhelmine Germany, and of imperial Great Britain, as well as catastrophic defeats for Napoleon, Nazi Germany, and the Soviet Union.

These confrontations have almost always resulted in intense security competition, which can yield hegemonic war. A review of the historical record reveals that hegemonic conflicts are relatively rare. Unfortunately, like major earthquakes, even if they are rare, their consequences are profound, woefully destructive, and lasting. The Peloponnesian War, the Punic Wars, the Thirty Years' War, the War of the Spanish Succession, the Seven Years' War, the French Revolutionary and Imperial wars, World War I and World War II, and the Cold War had lasting impacts on the international politics of the time. The ongoing conflict waged by the PRC against the US will as well.

But there is a caveat, and it is a big one. The fact that the logic of power politics fails after the Cold War, where the US aided the PRC's rise, is a historical anomaly. Of course, this strategically bizarre exception to power politics is the topic of this study. Such a unique occurrence, where the dominant great power aided and supported its challenger's rise, must be explained not by strategic reasoning in Washington, but by other factors. These include economic and financial considerations, and a strong political idealism that perceived a world without peer competitive threats to the United States. From Beijing's perspective, Deng's political warfare strategy of threat deflation succeeded beyond expectation and for far longer than he could have hoped.

Therefore, the absence of US balancing against the PRC demonstrates that the logic of power politics is an insufficient guarantee of a great power's security if its logic is dismissed, not understood, considered not relevant to the age, or, lamentably, if decision-makers are ignorant of its principles, history, consequences, and guidance. The principles of power politics, no matter how relevant to the strategic situation faced by the US, cannot assist statesmen as a guide to national security if they are discounted or not understood. That was the flaw of US decision-makers after the Cold War and, with regret, that error remains to be completely corrected.

Power Politics and the Sino-American Relationship During the Cold War

The US employed the logic of power politics to check Soviet power. Soviet conventional power and nuclear weapons threatened US security and the credibility of Washington's extended deterrent. To meet its obligations, it sought support from its allies, as well as to enlist Chinese support to balance Soviet might and to aid the end of the Vietnam War.

What the PRC provided the US was significant. First, Beijing permitted the US to locate intelligence bases on its soil after the end of US facilities based in Iran (TACKSMAN) after the Shah's fall in 1979.[9] Second, it also complicated Soviet defense planning by threatening the Soviet's eastern flank. From the 1960s, after the Sino-Soviet split, the Soviet Union faced a six front war problem: US strategic power, NATO, Great Britain and France's independent nuclear deterrents, Iran under the Shah and Islamic Revolution after his demise, Japan and US power in the Pacific, and China. As an aspect of this, from the 1970s, the PRC also served to occupy approximately forty-four Soviet divisions based on the Sino-Soviet border and was targeted by Soviet tactical, theater, and strategic nuclear forces.

The price the US paid for this entente was considerable. At the outset, Washington had to permit the PRC to occupy the Republic of China's UN Security Council seat in 1971. The US yielded to the PRC's demand to occupy China's seat with no *quid pro quo*, which established a protocol that continues even today. Nixon's February 1972 opening to the PRC is usually perceived a positive employment of power politics by Mao Zedong and Nixon to balance the growing Soviet threat. There is a good argument that it is so—the US wanted to employ the PRC to offset Soviet might.

However, it compels the question: might a better result have been achieved by maintaining support for the Republic of China (Taiwan), as Mao would be targeted by the Soviets even absent an entente with the US? It also provokes a strategic accounting—how much did the PRC actually contribute to the US in the Cold War with the Soviet Union? At different times, both Washington and Moscow were Beijing's main threat. The US was in the 1950s with the Korean War and the Taiwan Strait Crises of 1954–1955 and 1958. However, by the 1960s, even with the Vietnam War, the Soviets were a major threat to Beijing. The Sino-Soviet border clashes in 1968 and 1969, the construction by the Soviets of airfields in Mongolia, redeploying bombers from Eastern Europe to Soviet Central Asia, and Lin Biao's—Mao's expected successor—attempted 1971 *coup d'état* against Mao were reminders that the two Communist titans had profoundly competing ideological and geopolitical interests. In the summer of 1969, Nixon and Kissinger identified Soviet efforts to prepare an attack against the PRC. Each was a great threat to the other, and this ensured that Sino-Soviet enmity would be great and lasting. Nixon certainly believed he could capitalize upon this strategic calculus and hatred between the Communist giants.

Notwithstanding the key question of what precisely the PRC contributed, Nixon himself believed he needed an entente with the PRC to coerce North Vietnam to reach an agreement with the US and South Vietnam. But this record is mixed at best. In fact, the PRC never closed the rail line of communication from the Soviet Union to North Vietnam that allowed the Soviets to resupply the North. Additionally, Soviet, other Warsaw Pact, and neutral vessels always had access to the major port of Haiphong and the lesser port of Vinh until the Nixon administration's decision to mine those ports in May 1972, which underscored the importance of the rail lines.

Once the Paris Accords were signed and the US had exited the Vietnam War in March 1973, Vietnam receded in importance for the US. Yet Nixon's perception was that the PRC was still needed to balance Soviet power. The value of another front in the Cold War against the Soviets was seen as critical. The PRC did provide that; it could not avoid Soviet enmity whether it was allied with the US or not. The price the US paid was great in comparison with what it received.

The Ford administration continued to sustain the logic of power politics, as did the Carter administration. Carter's decision to recognize the PRC on January 1, 1979, while advancing the "One China" policy, thus yielding to Beijing's pressure on this issue, came at significant cost to the US. As Taipei was no longer recognized, the US lost that leverage over the PRC, as well as access to air and naval bases and integration with Taiwan defense forces. At the time, Taiwan remained shielded from invasion by the PRC's inability to execute an airborne or amphibious invasion or to implement a blockade of the island and sustain it until Taipei surrendered.

The benefits that the US received were important. As noted, the US gained the ability move the TACKSMAN stations to the PRC under operation CHESTNUT. The cost was sharing intelligence with the PRC.[10] Once recognized, the PRC had gained its remaining major diplomatic goal—this mission continues today as the PRC pressures states to recognize it rather than the Republic of China. The US also had to turn a blind eye to the Khmer Rouge's genocide in Cambodia. The PRC supported the Khmer Rouge and Prince Norodom Sihanouk during war with US-supported Lon Nol's government until its overthrow by the Khmer Rouge in 1975. The Khmer Rouge's genocide is estimated to have killed between 1.5 and 3 million Cambodians, about a quarter of Cambodia's 1975 population of 7.8 million, with the reverberations still being felt today as the PRC builds the Cambodian port of Ream for use by the People's Liberation Army Navy (PLAN).

Support for the UNITA (National Union for the Total Independence of Angola) guerrilla movement fighting the Soviet and Cuban-backed Communist MPLA (Popular Movement for the Liberation of Angola) government in Angola and the Soviet invasion of Afghanistan provided other points of cooperation in Sino-American relations. The PRC's aid to the Afghanis was limited to ammunition, light arms, heavy machine guns, mines, mortars, mules for transport, and diplomatic support. The US paid for the items and the PRC delivered them. PRC's support to the Afghan resistance provided another thorn in the side of Sino-Soviet relations and was in support of the Carter and Reagan administrations' backing of the Afghan guerrillas.

Additional points of cooperation were the arrival of Chinese students in the United States. The chance to study in the US quickly became the single most coveted privilege among young urban Chinese. The students landed so many jobs as laboratory and research assistants in STEM (Science, Technology, Engineering, and Mathematics) disciplines that they constituted a large portion of the universities' high-tech labor pool. Universities came to depend upon their Chinese graduate students and had a stake in preserving this status quo. The result was that Chinese students came to the US in far greater numbers than the Carter administration anticipated. This set the stage for unprecedented knowledge transfer to the PRC. The education of undergraduate and graduate students over decades, in essence, educated the enemy. It created the modern PRC university system in the STEM disciplines because many of their faculty were trained in the West, or by those trained there.

Over the decade after 1979, about 80,000 students and scholars came to the US, including Wang Huning, the author of the 1991 book *America Against America*. Today, Wang is a close ally of Xi Jinping and serves on the seven-member Politburo Standing Committee, the members of which were revealed at the Twentieth Party Congress held in mid-October 2022. The Politburo Standing Committee is the most powerful body within the Party, and Wang is the most significant ideologist for the Chinese regime. In his role, Wang is akin to that of Mikhail Suslov (who died in 1982) in the Communist Party of the Soviet Union (CPSU). Suslov was its chief ideologue, guardian of the purity of Communist ideology against Western influences, and in change of relations with foreign Communist parties. Whereas Suslov never visited the United States and indeed almost never met non-Communist Westerners, Wang lived in the United States from 1988–1989 during a six-month visit as a visiting scholar to over thirty cities and almost twenty universities.

Moreover, Carter approved the PRC's MFN trade status for the first time. Hence, of the two Communist titans, the PRC had MFN and the Soviet

Union did not. Warren Christopher, the Deputy Secretary of State asserted in the 1980: "It is in our interest for China's next generation leaders to look back in 1990 upon the relationship that we are now building with a sense of satisfaction and to view the United States as a reliable partner in development."[11]

Finally, PRC request for military technology was considered by Secretary of Defense Harold Brown in January 1980 where "non-lethal" aid was permitted to be sold to China including air defense radars, communications equipment, and transport helicopters. A ground station for Landsat satellites was also sold ostensibly for civilian purposes, but which amounted to a breakthrough for China's satellite reconnaissance program, giving Chinese military and intelligence officials the means to improve greatly the resolution of their satellites.[12] Later in September 1980, Undersecretary of Defense William Perry's delegation to Beijing and Chinese defense facilities considered further sales but these were not implemented before the end of the administration.[13]

A Rubicon had been crossed in the relationship between the US and the PRC. The PRC was a major Communist state, with whom the US had fought two wars, in Korea and also in Vietnam, where PLA units manned Anti-Aircraft Artillery (AAA) sites during the air war over North Vietnam during Operation Rolling Thunder (1965–1968).[14] PLA forces killed, wounded, and downed US aircraft and in turn were killed by attacks on those sites and transportation infrastructure. Many tens of thousands of Chinese workers helped to maintain North Vietnam's transport infrastructure.

Thus, a bit more than a decade before, the US and PRC forces were shooting at each other in North Vietnam. Two-and-a-half decades before, both were fighting a war in Korea. Now, the United States sold to the PRC what it had long sought: military hardware and advanced Western technology with military applications. Adhering to the logic of power politics, the US was selling to the PRC what it never would to the Soviet Union to help the PRC's military balance the shared threat of the USSR.

The Reagan administration was torn between Beijing and Taipei but ultimately continued the thrust of Carter's policy with added support for Taiwan. This was advanced through the 1982 Taiwan Defense Act, which resolved the issue of arms sales to Taiwan—the major issue unresolved by Carter and Deng when they concluded their agreement on normalization of relations at the end of 1978. In the last years of the Carter administration, the US had been selling about $500 million worth of arms to Taiwan. National Security Decision Directive (NSDD) 11 was signed by Reagan in 1981 and permitted the US to transfer advanced technology to the PRC's military to improve its combat effectiveness. In 1982, NSDD 12 facilitated cooperation in military and civilian nuclear matters.[15]

The PRC called the Reagan administration the "golden decade" due to the military technology transfer and the key step of opening of AMC's Jeep production facility in China. Now US firms were manufacturing in the PRC, which would never happen in the USSR.[16] While Carter had emphasized "nonlethal" military aid, Secretary of State Alexander Haig, leader of the pro-PRC faction, who struggled against National Security Advisor Richard Allen, National Security Council official and later (1981–1984) director of the American Institute in Taiwan James Lilley, and Defense Secretary Caspar Weinberger's pro-Taiwan faction, informed Deng in June 1981 that lethal aid would be sold.[17] Haig conveyed the invitation to People's Liberation Army's Vice Chief of Staff, Liu Hauqing, to Washington to discuss weapons purchases.[18] More importantly, in the summer of 1981, many alumni of the Carter administration traveled to the PRC.[19] Chinese officials were discovering that US politicians after they left office often sought to make money from their PRC connections, while recognizing that many of them still had significant influence in US business and politics. Moreover, they might return to US governmental service someday.

The tension was resolved when Haig resigned in July 1982. The August 17, 1982, communiqué (the Third Communiqué) on Taiwan was a major and controversial agreement with the PRC and became the foundation of the Six Assurances. The Reagan administration did not promise to end arms sales to Taiwan, as Beijing wanted, but did agree to set limits on those sales where none existed before. Reagan promised Taiwan that the US would not alter the Taiwan Relations Act; would not alter its position on Taiwan's sovereignty; would not consult with the PRC about the kinds of arms sold to Taiwan; the US would never try to mediate between China and Taiwan; and that the US would not pressure Taiwan to negotiate with the PRC. Reagan also immediately dictated a one-page memo to eviscerate secretly and unilaterally what he had signed.[20] Reagan stated that the US would restrict arms sales to Taiwan so long as the balance of military power between China and Taiwan was preserved.[21]

Fundamentally, as the Reagan policy towards Taiwan stabilized, Reagan's belief was that if the PRC became belligerent, or expanded its military and power projection capabilities to the point where regional stability was threatened, then the US would increase arms sales.[22] As Lilley states: "For Reagan, maintaining the balance of power across the Taiwan Strait had to be the departure point for US foreign policy."[23] As the threat to the island greatly expanded, the US would match those improvements to deter an invasion. Thus, Reagan's policy toward Taiwan was to have the ability to maintain a balance of power with the PRC and thereby have a conventional deterrent to a potential PRC attack.

Haig's replacement, George Shultz, believed that the PRC needed the US more than the US did the PRC. Shultz favored once again placing Japan as a key ally at the center of US attention in the Pacific for combating the Soviet threat. He also questioned whether the price that the US was paying for the entente with the PRC was worth what it had to pay, which was a good hardnosed question to ask.[24] Reagan visited the PRC in 1984 and a year later Chinese President Li Xiannian became the first formal head of state to visit the US, which was another sign of the positive relationship.

The Reagan years were different from the Nixon, Ford, and Carter years because cooperation with the PRC had been close but not deep. Throughout the 1970s, the relationship between the countries were constrained by the lack of diplomatic relations. By the early 1980s, the relationship deepened and flourished to the point where, although neither recognized it at the time, the decade would come to be viewed as the zenith of their relations. Knowing that tying the PRC to the Western economic system was critical for the CCP's interests, in 1986, the PRC joined the Asian Development Bank, and applied to join the General Agreement on Tariffs and Trade (GATT), although providentially this was not supported by the US at the time.

However, US military aid flowed to China. In June 1984, Reagan made the PRC eligible for the Department of Defense's Foreign Military Sales, which permitted the PRC to buy some weapons directly and with US financing of the purchase. The aperture was narrow but important given the PLA's weaknesses. This included US avionics upgrades on J-8II fighters, modelled on the MiG-21, called operation PEACE PEARL, and which were exported as the Shenyang F-8II.[25] At the same time, due to the PRC's arms sales to Iran and Iraq during their 1980–1988 war, arms proliferation became a major concern, especially Silkworm anti-ship cruise missiles after the May 1987 Reagan administration decision to re-flag Kuwaiti oil tankers. With this, they effectively became US ships and so entitled to the US Navy protection. PRC officials actually denied they had sold the missiles, and the lack of candor soured the goodwill that many in the US defense establishment had towards the PRC due to the fight against the mutual enemy of the Soviet Union.

In October 1987, the Reagan administration announced it would restrict the export of high technology to the PRC as a response to the missile sales.[26] Despite protests from the business community, within a few months the PRC promised to terminate the sale of future Silkworms to Iran, without admitting they had sold them. The subsequent revelation that the PRC had sold 36 intermediate range CSS-2 ballistic missiles to Saudi Arabia and had pledged to sell M-9 and M-11 missiles to Syria, with additional sales to Iran, Pakistan, and Libya showed that Beijing was engaged in missile proliferation despite US warnings. This pattern of behavior has been the consistent practice of the CCP, yet America's national security establishment, the permanent state, failed to detect it or to respond to this reality. The PRC was pursuing its own interests even when it violated US national security interests or threatened the security of the US military.

In what was a major success for the PRC, in 1988 Defense Secretary Frank Carlucci cleared the way for export licenses that would permit US-made commercial satellites to be launched in China on the Chinese Long March derived space launch vehicles. The United States had never before approved the launch of a US manufactured satellite by anyone other than Western allies. At the time, Hughes Aircraft, the maker of satellites that Asian and Australian firms sought to launch in China due to lower costs, lobbied intensively for the Reagan administration to approve the launches, over the opposition of General Dynamics and Martin Marietta, as this would undercut their prices for satellite launches.[27] For approving the PRC's launching of satellites, the Reagan administration received very little in return and exposed satellite technologies to capture by the PRC.

After Reagan, the George H.W. Bush administration got off to a difficult start in February 1989 when dissident and proponent of political liberalization and democratic reforms, Fang Lizhi, was invited by the US president to Bush's banquet in Beijing.[28] Frequently in Western media Fang was noted as the PRC's Andrei Sakharov, a Soviet dissident and, like Fang, a major physicist. The PRC employed the police to prevent Fang from attending the banquet. In the almost two decades of meetings at the highest levels between the PRC and the US there had never been such a brutal occasion. Deng had employed his secret police to prevent a Chinese citizen from attending a dinner as a guest of the US president. Moreover, PRC officials had thus rejected the negotiated compromise that led US officials to believe Fang would be present.[29]

Fundamentally, and this remains true today, the CCP regime was extraordinarily insecure and fearful about its hold on the Chinese people.[30] The Deng regime had insulted the Bush administration, and yet the Bush administration sought to cast blame on US ambassador Winston Lord. This is due in part, as investigative journalist James Mann argues, to Bush and National Security Advisor Brent Scowcroft basing their views of China largely on their experiences with the controlled society of the 1970s, not sensitive to how the population of Chinese cities had changed, particularly young people's demands for political reform in Beijing.[31] Broadly, the US had missed that the Deng regime would react with such fury to Fang's invitation, just as it would miss Deng's response to events at Tiananmen Square just four months later in June 1989.

As the Cold War continued, the Bush administration deserves credit for trying to sustain the Sino-American relationship on an even keel. There was sound logic for maintaining the PRC's role in the balance of power. Soviet General Secretary Mikhail Gorbachev's visit to Beijing in May 1989 was a sharp reminder that Gorbachev understood power politics.[32] Gorbachev failed to make headway with Japan, promising return of the "Northern Territories" for Japanese neutralization, or with West Germany, where once again the appeal to Chancellor Helmut Kohl was German unification in exchange for West Germany leaving NATO and the neutralization of a united Germany. The

PRC offered Gorbachev a chance to stabilize his eastern front, reduce defense spending in favor of economic reforms, and improve relations with the CCP. Since Nixon's presidency, Washington was fearful that Beijing and Moscow would return to their early-Cold War entente that would have increased the threat to the US and its allies. A successful mission by Gorbachev might once again move Beijing into the Soviet camp and would mark the return of an intense and dangerous Cold War for the US.

Gorbachev was a charismatic leader who needed to improve Sino-Soviet relations. Soviet forces were withdrawing from Afghanistan, and Gorbachev had pledged to unilaterally remove most of the Soviet forces on the Sino-Soviet border. His visit to Beijing passed without major changes as Deng—with an eye to the sharp realities of geopolitics—was certain Gorbachev was in a position of weakness. He saw that far more could be gained from the West in the 1990s than from a terminally ill Soviet Union.

The death of Hu Yaobang, the former CCP General Secretary who had been ousted two years earlier, on April 15, 1989, started a series of student protests in and around Tiananmen Square.[33] Students and others came first to lay wreaths in Hu's honor at the base of the Monument to People's Heroes. From several thousand in the Square, the protest grew to tens of thousands, and then over a 100,000, and then to about 500,000 when Gorbachev arrived on May 15, 1989. It reached a million days after. The Tiananmen Square protests overshadowed the Gorbachev visit or the port calls to Shanghai made by 7th Fleet vessels USS *Blue Ridge*, *Sterett*, and *Rodney M. Davis* to take some wind out of the Soviet's sails and underscore Sino-American military cooperation in the face of Gorbachev's visit.[34]

Bush's efforts to warn Deng off the crackdown through private messages showed that when it mattered, Bush's relationship with Deng would not stop Deng acting in his interests to save the CCP. "Our backs are to the wall," noted President Yang Shangkun, a close ally of Deng, while Deng said, "if we retreat any further we're done for."[35] Lilley had studied Deng for almost three decades, and his assessment was that although Deng was "the father of China's economic liberalization, he was a dyed-in-the-wool Communist, committed to using force to restore order."[36] On June 9, Deng made his first appearance since the massacre. He was firm: "The aim of the small group of counterrevolutionary rebels was to overthrow the Communist Party, the socialist system, and the PRC in order to set up a bourgeois republic."[37] He would never yield. This was another seminal and lasting event that demonstrated the strategic foolishness of shaping the PRC through the personal relationships US leaders might have with their CCP counterparts.

The tepid, bordering on indifferent, response by the Bush administration to the Tiananmen Square massacre on June 3–4, 1989, and the Scowcroft secret mission to Beijing June 30–July 1, 1989, was intended to assure Deng that the US wanted to preserve the relationship. A second secret Scowcroft mission went in December 1989, following up on separate visits Nixon and Kissinger had taken in the autumn of 1989.

The window of vulnerability for the CCP lasted for some time. The PRC's economy was fragile in the two years after Tiananmen. The Japanese government had suspended a package of $5.6 billion in loans to the PRC after the massacre, and the World Bank froze more than $2 billion in new interest-free loans. If there ever was a time when the US held considerable economic leverage over the PRC, this was it. But the administration did not employ this leverage, and gradually all returned to the *status quo ante*. Within a couple of years, Deng succeeded spectacularly by reviving the PRC's economic growth, and the moment of US economic leverage had passed.[38]

Had the US decided, the immediate wake of Tiananmen would have been an opportunity to push the CCP hard in the expectation that it would fall from power. Biting sanctions and diplomatic pressure could have been brought to bear against the CCP. At a minimum, Bush might have pressed to ensure that it was permanently delegitimized as a remnant Communist state. The US had formidable capability at the time, a product of its two major war preparations and formidable political warfare capabilities to hurt the CCP. It also possessed an understanding of Communism and the inherent aggressiveness of that ideology that US decision-makers lost in the decades after.

Although it is painful to acknowledge today in light of the rise of the PRC, the Bush administration's desire to sustain positive relations with the PRC was a logical response to uncertainty within the Soviet Union and the need to sustain the anti-Soviet entente with the PRC. The Soviet Union would remove itself from the calculus of the balance of power after the collapse of the August 1991 *coup d'état* against Gorbachev and the rise of Boris Yeltsin as a viable Russian nationalist alternative to the rule of the Communist Party of the Soviet Union. Although Russia would remain an important military power due to its large nuclear capabilities, it was removed from primary consideration in the calculus of power politics.

Japanese power was also a concern. Although Japan was a close and democratic ally, as Soviet power weakened and then collapsed, and the PRC was not capable of challenging the US, nor was India, the Japanese-American alliance might weaken or terminate due to the lack of threat to sustain it. The relative power of Japan vis-à-vis the US made Japan a concern for reasons of power politics. In a possible future where the US-Japanese relationship soured, the PRC would be a counterweight to Japan.

In addition, the administration was uncertain whether the CCP could sustain its rule in China. The demise of Communist governments in 1989 and the Soviet Union after December 1991 permitted the administration to consider alternative potential futures for the CCP, including where the CCP had fallen, or where Deng had been overthrown and new leadership in place. Uncertainty about the staying power of Deng and the CCP broadly colored the Bush administration's consideration of the tools that it had to influence that outcome and the value of the CCP under Deng's leadership to balance other power considerations in Asia.[39] But the ability of the US to act waned as the CCP's rule over the Chinese people stabilized in the years after the massacre.

Fundamentally, the PRC was not as great a concern in the aftermath of Communism's end in Central and Eastern Europe, and the Soviet Union tribulations between the summer of 1989 and the August 1991 unsuccessful *coup d'état* and its aftermath. The Bush administration did not have the time, energy, or resources to devote to China as its relative power, and the dangers the PRC posed at that time were small in comparison to those imposed by German unification, the revolutions of 1989, the Soviet Union's turmoil and breakup, and the First Gulf War—Operations Desert Shield/Desert Storm 1990–1991. The situation in the PRC was loaded with risks and profound uncertainty, and a peaceful demise was not guaranteed. Additionally, the PRC was so weak at the time, it could not affect the distribution of power or even act as a great power to defeat US global national security interests.

At about 1.6 percent of world's gross domestic product, the PRC was only a modest threat to the US. The danger to Taiwan was not forgotten; in fact, 150 advanced F-16 fighters were approved for sale, which was in response to the PRC's purchase from Russia of advanced surface-to-air missiles, Kilo-class submarines, and sophisticated SU-27 fighters, which changed the balance of power between Beijing and Taipei.[40]

The PRC's support for the First Gulf War at the UN allowed Bush to overturn Saddam Hussein's aggression against Kuwait. This seemed to confirm the wisdom of Scowcroft's mission to preserve the relationship with the PRC. Overturning Iraq's aggression was an immediate and significant priority for the Bush administration. Thus, the change in the distribution of power in favor of the US led to a unique condition where the US had its "unipolar moment," and an exaggerated influence in international politics as there was no superpower—the Soviet Union was gone—or even a great power, that could check its influence.

The "End of History"

The free elections in Poland in June 1989 and limited free elections in Hungary, four free by-elections in July, coupled with East Germany's granting of permission for its citizens to travel to Hungary—which had de-militarized its border with Austria and thus provided East Germans with an avenue of escape—were the start of the political events behind the Iron Curtain that heralded its end. 1989 was an epochal year in world politics. 1989 was also effervescent intellectually. Francis Fukuyama advanced the idea that Western liberal democracy had established its superiority and so yielded a Hegelian "End of History" moment.

For Fukuyama's Hegelian perspective, Hegel's "spirit" (*Geist*) had been revealed through a dialectical process to reveal that democratic government and capitalism will be an eternal norm. In essence, the world had learned what the best political and economic systems were, and it was only a matter of time before states came to this realization and so adopted liberal democracy and capitalism.

As Fukuyama argued: "The triumph of the West, of the Western *idea* is evident first of all in the total exhaustion of viable systematic alternative to

Western liberalism."[41] He continued, "in the past decades, there have been particular period [*sic*] of postwar history, but the end of history as such: that is, the end point of mankind's ideological evolution and the universalization of Western liberal democracy as the final form of human government."[42]

The ideas that Fukuyama advanced were impactful for four major reasons. First, his timing was excellent, and the ideas of the article spread widely as each day seemed to confirm its logic and provide more empirical evidence in support of his argument. The revolutions that swept Europe and were attempted in China, and the demise of the Soviet Union seemed to answer the question. The adoption of democracy and capitalism by the states of Central and Eastern Europe in the 1990s seemed to confirm History's march. Fukuyama was right.

Second, the work flattered the West. It was the West that developed these ideas and so its *amour propre* was confirmed as the rest of the world came to the same conclusions. This contributed to a conceit among Western intellectuals, politicians, foundations, and media, that the West was the apotheosis of History. In turn, this fueled a rationale for spreading democracy using coercive diplomacy and force—to aid History along. Accordingly, the Western involvement in Russia's reform and economic "shock treatment" of the 1990s, in the wars of Yugoslavia and Kosovo, and the desire to build democracy in Afghanistan after 9/11 and in Iraq after 2003 were informed by Fukuyama's argument.

Third, the work had policy implications that dovetailed with senior national security decision-makers preferences of the time. In his State of the Union address of January 1994, President Bill Clinton had identified the democratic peace—the theory that democratic states will not fight one another—as a law of social science and was instrumental to the Clinton administration's strategy of "Democratic Enlargement."[43] This view was shared by UK Prime Minister Tony Blair and Foreign Minister Jack Straw during NATO's Allied Force against Serbia in 1999—which was proclaimed by its advocates as the first progressive war for democracy and human rights. Accordingly, advancing democracy in the western Balkans, Haiti, or in Russia and the states of the former Soviet Union was advancing the cause of peace and of human rights while allowing those countries to yield to the demands of the liberal international order. For many Western politicians and analysts, there was no question that the PRC would be brought along by the tides of Hegelian History too. After all, the four "Asian Tigers," Hong Kong, Singapore, South Korea, and Taiwan had made the transition from authoritarianism to democracy, so Western leaders were confident the PRC would as well.

The George W. Bush administration shared a similar conception of the stabilizing role of democracy. One of the rationales for invading Iraq in 2003 was that a democratic Iraq would foster the success of democracy in the Middle East and serve as a beacon for other Middle Eastern states to follow the same path.

Fourth, the idea soaked into the Western national security culture and was reflected in the beliefs of foreign policy decision-makers and influencers at the Council on Foreign Relations and other major think tanks, philanthropic foundations, Western media, and academics. The curriculum of the War Colleges reflected the idea.[44] Moreover, due to the "death of distance" as a result of the internet, web, and other technological innovations, goods could be made and services could be provided anywhere, so globalization was going to provide global efficiencies in manufacturing and permit just in time delivery that was a fillip to investors and Wall Street. The cost of globalization was considerable. It included hollowing out American manufacturing power and countless American communities. Advancing liberal democracy also meant furthering human rights, including women's rights, and the tenets of globalization. The domestic implications of Fukuyama's thesis manifested itself by promises of a "peace dividend," and the Clinton Administration began to dismantle the Reagan era buildup of America's military power. Thus, there was bipartisan support as well as a broad coalition of support from Non-Governmental Organizations (NGOs) that wanted to employ this reasoning to sweep into History's dustbin patriarchal states and destroy traditional, oppressive cultures to advance the rights of women and ethnic and sexual minorities.

Therefore, the influence of the idea of the "End of History" is difficult to minimize. The consequence was to disarm Western national security decision-makers to the ideological motivations for conflict that the CCP possessed and still does. It provided the CCP with a tool to employ to deceive national security decision-makers, as they could entice them to believe that political reform was "just around the corner" as it inevitably followed economic reform. Indeed, perhaps most perniciously, it provided support for the pro-CCP school. If Fukuyama's thesis was right, then it was incumbent for Western decision-makers to support engagement with China, fostering investment and cooperation, to further economic and so, in time, political democratization in the PRC. Consequently, Fukuyama's thesis provided the logic for the pro-CCP school to ground its arguments. That logic seemed to accord with the empirical evidence around the world: democracy was on the march.

Of course, History did not end, and the West was compelled to recognize that rather than being teleological, it is cyclical. States are always rising and falling due to changes in the distribution of power that, in turn, is as a result of varying rates of economic growth or economic decline.[45] Simply because the United States was dominant does not mean that it always will be, as power is redistributed in international politics. There are only Ten Commandants, so we know that Eleventh Commandant is not that the US will always be omnipotent. If History is teleological, it may be that its end is Communism as advanced by the CCP. If it is cyclical, then every hegemon or potential hegemon will believe that its ideology is best and defines History's terminus.

In sum, Fukuyama's argument should be considered a representation of political liberalism—even an inspiration for today's progressive movement. Americans and their leaders have often viewed international politics through a teleological prism. For political liberals, war was a problem that can be solved through good ideology or good economic systems or both. Liberalism is teleological, states are moving toward these good ends. If states are democratic and free market, then their shared beliefs will keep them from conflict. Democracy and free market capitalism were the highest forms of political and economic organization. Woodrow Wilson entered World War I to make the world safe for democracy. The nineteenth century free market economist Frédéric Bastiat said "when goods do not cross borders, armies will," and his observation well captured the liberal belief that trade causes peace. Fukuyama's argument resonated powerfully with the American elite. Its innate liberalism even more than Hegelianism contributed to its warm reception among US policy-makers and academics.

The Sino-American Relationship After the Cold War: Engagement Bests Power Politics

With the demise of the Soviet Union and its ability to compel US decision-makers to maintain the calculus of power politics as foremost in their minds, that disciplinary force faded from importance. "End of History" reasoning and the financial and pecuniary benefits of investing in China were at the fore by the mid-1990s. The intellectual change for the national security community was rapid. It turned from the geopolitical necessity of balancing peer competitors to, in essence, doing what the US wanted without fear of an adversary, or group of adversaries, to check US power. The March 1992 leak to the *New York Times* of the draft Defense Policy Guidance (DPG) for the 1994–1999 fiscal years dated February 18, 1992, was one of the last warnings of the seriousness of great power competition.[46] The draft's call for the US to remain dominant and prevent the emergence of another rival, whether Russia or elsewhere, was a valuable strategic insight that might have generated strategies tailored to dissuade, prevent, or delay the PRC's growth.

Implicitly, the draft DPG was in accord with the logic of power politics. Great powers rise and fall and there is never a "time out" in international politics. Unless husbanded carefully, power will be redistributed as economic growth rates, and thus relative power is constantly changing. It is certainly worth considering whether the US might have maintained its position if subsequent administrations had heeded its insights. The greatest threat to US security would have been avoided and the PRC's deleterious impact on the American people and US national security interests would have been prevented.

The Clinton administration was the first of the post-Cold War period when the US did not confront a peer and the PRC did not have the capabilities to challenge the US military power, so the US could employ its military might in support of lesser missions. These included the mission in Somalia in support of the UN, enforcing the "no fly" zones in Iraq, faced the regional threats of Iran and North Korea, balancing Serb power in Bosnia-Herzegovina by supporting Bosnian Muslims and Croats, and deterring ethnic cleansing of Hungarians in Vojvodina, Albanians in Kosovo, and Serb aggression against the Former Yugoslav Republic of Macedonia, and stabilizing Haiti.

The first two years of the Clinton presidency were defined by the positive action of linking the PRC's human rights record to the renewal of MFN.[47] China's MFN benefits were at the very core of the economic relationship between the two countries. With MFN status, the PRC could trade with the United States on the same basis as almost every other country in the world. Without MFN, Chinese products would be subject to barriers to trade, including duties so high that it would be difficult to sell them in the enormous US market.

In the decade since Congress first approved President Carter's extension of MFN status to the PRC in 1980, those trade benefits had been quietly renewed for another year, with the expectation that it would always be so. Nevertheless, the PRC as a Communist country was subject to the provision of the Jackson-Vanik Amendment, which required that the president formally renew the benefits each year. Congress could reject a presidential decision if it wanted to do so. The deadline for the presidential decision was June of each year. In the immediate wake of Tiananmen, they had been quietly renewed for another year.

The optics of this were bad. For the Bush administration, it was occasionally difficult for Washington to explain why the US favored Beijing over Moscow, which did not have MFN, at a time when Gorbachev was attempting reforms and had abandoned much of the Soviet empire, while the Tiananmen crackdown showed the PRC's tyranny. If Communist states were destined for the "ash heap of history," this would have been a propitious time to give the CCP a push.

In March 1990, Representative Nancy Pelosi (D-CA) formed a new congressional working group on the PRC aimed at opposing Bush's policies on China.[48] In 1990, the earliest skirmish in Congress over MFN benefits, the Chinese students in the US were a strong influence in Congress. Soon they would vanish from the MFN debate. The American business community at first was rather weak and modestly represented. Only toy manufactures and the National Association of Wheat Growers appeared at the first testimony in May 1990. American businesses were slow of foot at the outset, but they would quickly become the dominant constituency in the annual MFN debates through the end of the Bush and early Clinton administrations.

Tibet was a thorny issue at the time as it had prominent actors supporting the Tibetan people. Soon Tibetan organizations put pressure on Pelosi
to add to her legislation linking human rights in Tibet to MFN benefits,
which Pelosi rejected in 1990 but approved in 1991. Eventually almost every
group and organization with an interest in the PRC wanted to have a voice
in drafting the specific MFN conditions. While Pelosi's preference would be
to keep MFN language focused on human rights, Senator Joe Biden (D-DE)
demanded that MFN contain requirements for the PRC to reduce tangibly
its weapons proliferation that benefited many states, including Libya, Iran,
Pakistan, and Syria. MFN issue was becoming the focal point of the efforts by
Congress to influence US policy toward the PRC.

Throughout the 1992 presidential campaign, Clinton was outspoken in
denouncing the Bush administration's approach to China. Clinton's most
famous words were those of his acceptance speech at the Democratic National
Committee in New York City in July, where he promised "an America that
will not coddle dictators from Baghdad to Beijing." Specifically, the Clinton
campaign was in accord with Democratic Party's leadership and Congressional
majority. He called for the imposition of a series of conditions the PRC would
have to meet for any annual renewals of MFN.

On the PRC, Clinton received an almost miraculous gift from the previous generations of American strategists who provided it due to their acumen
and statesmanship. Clinton came into office as the first president for whom
the distribution of power was benign due to the asymmetric imbalance in the
favor of the US. As a result, the "End of History" also permeated the national
security community with important exceptions like Andrew Marshall, the
Director of the Office of Net Assessment, and the authors of the draft DPB
that was leaked to the *New York Times*, who understood that such a distribution of power would only be in the US's favor temporarily. Inevitably new
peers would rise, and their intentions would be hostile to US national security
interests. If the US stood by and did not take effective countermeasures, the
US would once again face an intensely competitive geopolitical environment.

The Clinton administration altered Bush's policy of MFN renewal in two
respects. First, it dropped the language holding the PRC to account on proliferation. Second, it weakened the human rights language. Chinese students

had wanted Clinton's MFN order to include a provision requiring Beijing to release "all political prisoners" held as a result of the Tiananmen crackdown. The Clinton administration negotiated with Congress to delete the word "all." As negotiations continued, what attracted little notice at the time, but it turned out to be critical step, Clinton administration would employ executive orders and Congress dropped legislation. The Chinese students elected not to criticize the step. This might have signaled a lack of trust in the Clinton administration to enforce its own order. The administration had accomplished a subtle act: it dissuaded Congress from writing into law the very position of MFN conditionality that Clinton had endorsed in the campaign and was enshrined in his executive order. At the time, such congressional action seemed unnecessary.

A year later, Clinton did an about-face. This had a colossal impact as it was one of the key elements of the PRC's growth. Clinton's action rested upon the notion that the PRC would be willing to negotiate over the human rights conditions rather than simply defy the executive order.[49] The reasonable expectation of the Clinton administration was that over the next year, there would be discussions on the issue. Based on the PRC's behavior the previous two years, this was eminently reasonable because in the last two years of the Bush administration, the PRC had showed the willingness to make key compromises on human rights. As the congressional vote approached, the PRC would release dissidents and signal or actually make other concessions in order to help Bush avoid defeat on Capitol Hill.[50] But what was true of the past was no longer the case.

As Mann argues, this logic was faulty for four major reasons.[51] First, the good cop/bad cop approach between a Republican president and Democratic Congress put far more pressure on Beijing. Second, Clinton neglected to generate active support from the business community or the economic wing of his administration. Third, the penalties were Draconian. If the PRC did not yield, it would lose all its MFN trade benefits, an outcome that alarmed US businesses as well as the PRC. Fourth, in issuing his MFN order, Clinton was giving the PRC an ultimatum. Before doing so, he needed to be sure that he had the resolve to carry out the ultimatum. It was Clinton's responsibility to decide in advance whether he would follow through on his threat to cut off the PRC's trade benefits. If not, he should not have issued the order. There is little indication that in May 1993 Clinton confronted this issue, but soon he would.

US businesses interests were pushing for ever greater presence in the PRC. In the early months of 1993, US Ambassador to the PRC J. Stapleton Roy noticed that US businesses were flooding into the PRC.[52] He had not witnessed much interest when he came to Beijing two years before. In 1993, leader American corporations were coming to the PRC eager to start ventures. 1993 was a banner year for investment in the PRC from the US and the world. In 1993, the PRC signed 83,437 new contracts with foreign companies, worth $111 billion in new investments, and more than 6,700 of these contracts were with US companies. No other country in the world was attracting such capital.[53]

The dramatic increases in new investment started in 1992 and continued for decades. As described in detail below, in early 1992 Deng staged his final political comeback by promoting the PRC's opening to massive foreign investment to tie influential Westerners to the PRC's growth, and thus Western governments would support the CCP. The PRC's growth was astonishing—from a little more than four percent in 1990, to more than 12 percent in 1992, and almost 14 percent in 1993.[54]

In two years, the PRC had become the fastest growing economy in the world and businesses sought to capitalize on the environment Deng created by manufacturing their products where labor wages were Dickensian, and the government would ensure there were no strikes or other forms of labor unrest. By 1992, Japanese firms were rushing to invest in the PRC ahead of their South Korean competitors. Seeing this, European and US firms were trying to gain an edge on the Japanese with a "devil take the hindmost" attitude toward investment and trade with the PRC.

The implications of the PRC's growth for Clinton's MFN policy were profound. China had a vastly greater ability to withstand the threat of US sanctions in 1993 than it had had three years earlier. The pressures from US businesses and the economic wing of the Clinton administration to sustain open trade with the PRC were much more intense and successful.

This was critical and defined the ability of the PRC to rise to become the threat it is today. Clinton's tough approach on human rights might have worked immediately after the Tiananmen Square massacre. This is when the PRC's economy was fragile and US business interest in China was at its nadir. But power politics dictated cooperation against the Soviet Union.

If the Cold War had ended sooner, the US could have placed considerable pressure on the CCP. Or, if Clinton had been willing to place strategic interests before finance and economics—but this was supremely difficult to accomplish when he realized the Democrat Party, its candidates, and his own reelection bid, could benefit politically from it. The US national security community had internalized Fukuyama's "End of History" thesis: great power conflict had been banished to the history books along with gentlemen dueling at dawn to resolve matters of honor. If US firms and investors would not profit from Deng's openness, then Japanese, South Korean, and European firms would.

In August 1993, the tensions in Clinton's policy came to the fore when the administration said it would impose sanctions on the PRC for the sale of M-11 ballistic missile parts to Pakistan.[55] Pressure arose from California's Congressional delegation and Hughes Aircraft and Martin Marietta, which had contracts for the launch of communications satellites on Chinese space launch vehicles, were vulnerable to the sanctions. The administration backed off. For the Chinese leadership, the controversy showed that the Clinton administration was more vulnerable to commercial pressure than its predecessors and that it adopted policies it was unwilling to sustain.

In 1994, the rhetoric of the administration began to change through Ron Brown as Secretary of Commerce. The argument he made was that the best way to promote human rights was to encourage market reform and trade.[56] Moreover, and stunningly given the PRC threat today, Brown advanced unconditional MFN for the PRC as a matter of "economic security" and vital for US national security. Permanent Normal Trade Relations (PNTR), unconditional MFN, with the PRC was achieved.[57] This was a turning point in history and would ensure that Beijing would receive the rocket fuel for its economy that it needed.

There was significant tension in the Clinton administration between National Security Advisor Anthony Lake, who was the strongest proponent among senior administration officials for vigorous policies to advance human rights in the PRC, versus his deputy Sandy Berger, and the economic wing of the administration, including Brown, Assistant to the President for Economic Policy and Director of the National Economic Council Robert Rubin, and Secretary of the Treasury Lloyd Bentsen.[58] In 1995, Rubin would succeed Bentsen as Secretary of the Treasury.

While the debate between efforts to coerce the PRC or to work with it, that is, to engage with the CCP in the effort to change its policies did not start with Clinton administration, it was resolved with the Clinton presidency in favor of engagement. The pro-CCP school of thought would last until the Trump presidency began to change that orientation of the US government with some, although not complete, success.

In May 1994, Clinton stated that it was time to take a new path. The result of which was that the PRC won two victories.[59] First, the administration agreed to extend MFN to China in 1994 and in the future without conditions. Second, it backed away from imposing penalties upon China for its unwillingness to meet the conditions Clinton imposed for the 1993–1994 year. The Chinese had repeatedly argued that the MFN linkage was counterproductive for advancing human rights in the PRC as they could never make changes in response to US pressure. But the PRC did not change when the pressure was removed, either. The PRC had called Clinton's bluff. The administration would back down from the threats it made regarding human rights when its commercial interests were jeopardized.

Even the Taiwan Strait crisis was ostensibly generated by Taiwanese President Lee Teng-hui's private visit to provide the commencement address at his alma mater Cornell University in June 1995. In July 1995, the PRC fired ballistic missiles into the East China Sea while conducting military exercises. During Clinton's first two and a half years in office, the administration had been obliged to retreat for its policies on the PRC.[60] The first was on MFN and second was on Lee's visit, which the administration did not support. In the summer of 1995, the PRC was threatening military force against Taiwan. Taiwan's first direct presidential election was on March 23, 1996, with Lee as the KMT (Kuomintang, or Nationalist Party of China) candidate against the Democratic Progressive Party (DPP).

The PRC's military operations in the summer of 1995 were aimed at punishing Lee and the Clinton administration. However, the PLA's larger exercises and missile firings in March 1996, just before the election, prompted Clinton to send the USS *Independence* and later the USS *Nimitz* through the Taiwan Strait. In addition, a new defense agreement with Japan, which extended and broadened Washington's relationship with Tokyo, was announced.

As Clinton headed into the 1996 election, he had no other trouble from Beijing. The PRC leaders could see that the administration had been chastised by the earlier difficulties. Clinton did not intend to challenge Beijing as he had with the MFN policy of 1993–1994 and with the visa to President Lee. The PRC was not a major issue of the presidential campaign. During the autumn of 1996, the Clinton administration dispatched a new team of US trade negotiators to explore the possibility of a securing the PRC's entry into the WTO. WTO membership mattered because it would help advance the PRC's trade, augment its prestige, and be a tangible symbol of the Clinton administration's policy of integrating the PRC into the world's decision-making to provide it with a stake in the liberal international order. As Clinton declared in 1997, the PRC "was on the wrong side of history," but economic growth in the PRC would help to "increase the spirit of liberty over time. . . . I just think it's inevitable, just as inevitably the Berlin Wall fell."[61] A clear indicator of the power that the pro-CCP school of thought had achieved since Kissinger's first visit to the PRC in 1971 to set the stage for Nixon's visit in 1972.

Although WTO talks were delayed by the PRC's reluctance to make as many trade concessions as the administration sought, Deng's death at age 92 on February 19, 1997, and the political environment in Washington was not advantageous due to Congressional investigations into Chinese influence in the Clinton campaign's fundraising. Yet, the PRC remained on the glide-path to the WTO. In his final year in office, Clinton succeeded in ushering through Congress approved for the PRC's WTO membership. Clinton promised repeatedly that the PRC's WTO membership "is likely to have a profound impact on human rights and political liberty" in the PRC.[62]

As human rights receded, there was acerated cooperation in defense-related industries. In February 1996, a Chinese space launch vehicle exploded, destroying its payload, which was a Loral Corporation satellite. Experts from Loral Space and Communications Corp. and Hughes Electronics Corp. aided PRC officials to discover the cause of the failure. This was done without approval from the US government. There were also concerns that some of the satellite's technology was also compromised. In 1998, Loral was able to work with the PRC in another satellite launch, to which the Department of Justice objected as it hindered the prosecution of the 1996 case.[63] But the administration overrode the Department of Justice's concern.[64] In 2002, Loral paid a $14 million fine for violating the Arms Export Control Act, and Hughes paid $32 million in 2003.

These matters did not prevent Jiang Zemin from visiting the US in October 1997, when at a press conference Clinton declared the PRC to be on the wrong side of history. Neither did it prevent President Clinton from visiting the PRC in June 1998. However, the tremendous strain on Sino-American relations due to the mistaken bombing of the PRC's embassy in Belgrade during Allied Force in 1999 generated a vociferous anti-American reaction. It had a lasting effect as the CCP was able to exploit it to shape the Chinese people's perception of the US as a threat.

Most significantly, this was a time of epochal change, and the principles of power politics were ignored. The PRC's entry into the Western economic ecosystem was made possible. During the Cold War, US business interests were subordinate to the concerns of power politics. Now, under Clinton, commerce became the dominant driver of US foreign policy vis-à-vis the PRC. This transformation reflected the changing distribution of power in the US's favor and an administration that chose trade, commerce, and investment in the PRC over human rights and the fundamental strategic national security interests of the US. The unprecedented upsurge in foreign investment in the PRC gave it greater leverage than it had in the past. Majorities in Congress also supported Clinton's agenda.

During the second Clinton term, there was action in the Republican Congress. In the Senate, under Fred Thompson (R-TN), in 1997, a Governmental Affairs Committee investigated the PRC's influence in the 1996 US presidential and congressional elections. In particular, the Committee examined the activities of major Democratic bundler John Huang, who collected some $3.4 million dollars for the Democratic Party before scrutiny of foreign donations caused him to return about half of that amount.[65] The Committee also documented an FBI investigation of illegal campaign funding operation run from the PRC's embassy in Washington, DC. In its final report published in March 1998, the Thompson Committee concluded that the PRC directly attempted to influence the 1996 presidential and congressional elections.

In the House of Representatives, the Select Committee on US National Security and Military/Commercial Concern with the People's Republic of China, more commonly known as the Cox Commission after Chairman Christopher Cox (R-CA), investigated the PRC's technology acquisition in the 1980s and 1990s. The Committee's findings and recommendations were published in the Cox Report in May 1999. The Cox Commission revealed that the PRC stole design information related to seven of the US's nuclear weapons, which enabled in PRC to advance rapidly its warhead and Multiple Independently Targetable Reentry Vehicle (MIRV) design. This allowed the PRC to have modern designs that added the regime's confidence in their arsenal due to its increased reliability. Stealing the US nuclear secrets saved the tremendous costs of research, design, development and testing, and range of their missiles. The Cox Commission noted that for decades the Ministry of State Security (MSS) had placed priority on successfully targeting US National Laboratories, including nuclear weapon design at Los Alamos and Lawrence Livermore, and nuclear weapon engineering at Sandia. Regrettably, the Cox Report submitted that major security problems remained at the national laboratories. The report generated exceptional recommendations such as the creation of the National Nuclear Security Administration (NNSA) but not all were acted upon.[66]

Consequently, the entente in the Sino-American relationship that was originally aimed at the Soviet Union survived the end of the Cold War, even in the realm of military cooperation. Also in the Cold War, the US opened its markets to Chinese goods, encouraged American firms to invest in China, and granted the country MFN status. It thus developed commercial ties broader than with any other Communist country. These efforts were done with the hope of strengthening the PRC as an ally against the Soviet Union, and helped it become a more prosperous and powerful state. In the early 1990s, US firms became eager to do business with Beijing, which Clinton facilitated, essentially removing any barriers over human rights, Tibet, the need for regime change and democratic political reforms so that money could flow into the PRC and from the PRC to the coffers of political influence of the United States and other Western states.

The George W. Bush administration had similar motivations. On the campaign trail in November 1999, Bush had argued, that trade with the PRC "is not just monetary, but moral . . . Economic freedom creates habits of liberty. And habits of liberty create expectations of democracy . . . Trade freely with China and time is on our side."[67]

Once in office, the April 1, 2001, the collision by a PLA Air Force jet fighter into an unarmed reconnaissance turboprop aircraft, the EP-3E incident, created a crisis, which only reinforced Defense Secretary Donald Rumsfeld's great concerns over the growth of the PLA and the PRC's expanding kinetic and non-kinetic power.[68] But in the wake of 9/11, considered below, US foreign policy was dominated by the campaign in Afghanistan and by the need to have the PRC's acquiescence at the UN Security Council. The Bush administration needed a quiet, stable working relationship with the PRC. On Iraq, President Bush sided with the hawks, principally Vice President Richard Cheney and Deputy Secretary of Defense Paul Wolfowitz. On the PRC, he sided with the doves—the Engagers—so US support for the PRC's economy, economic and military growth, and of the CCP, continued unaffected. It seemed nothing could stop US trade and investment in the PRC.

The George W. Bush administration's vision for the PRC was described by Deputy Secretary of State Robert Zoellick in a 2005 address that should rival British Prime Minister Neville Chamberlain as a hopeful expression before disaster. He famously urged Beijing "to become a responsible stakeholder" in world politics. "China's actions—combined with a lack of transparency—can create risks," he declared.[69] In addition, "uncertainties about how China will use its power will lead the United States . . . to hedge relations with China." Of course, US officials hoped that Beijing would turn out to be benign, "but none will bet their future on it." Consequently, if the PRC wanted to improve US–China relations, it must "openly explain its defense spending, intentions, doctrine, and military exercises." The mere "idea of a 'peaceful rise,'" Zoellick noted, was not enough to allay US mistrust.

The Department of Defense took a similar position in the 2006 Quadrennial Defense Review (QDR). It stated that: "The outside world has little knowledge of Chinese motivations and decision-making. . . . The United States encourages China to take actions to make its intentions clear and clarify its military plans."[70] Understandably, despite Zoellick's plea to become a "responsible stakeholder," neither his nor the QDR's warnings had any effect on the PRC. Its expansionist behavior continued in accordance with its national agenda to restore the PRC to what they claimed was their historic and rightful place as a great power.

Any effort to address the PRC threat was derailed by terrible and shocking 9/11 terrorist attacks and the subsequent deployment and invasion of Iraq. These events occupied the large majority of the US national security community well into the Obama administration. The impact of 9/11 was profound for many reasons, including on American society and politics. But one of the weighty international costs was the time it provided the PRC to expand without an effective US response. The gift of time is one of the most precious in global politics, and the United States provided it to the PRC.

The Role of 9/11

Tragically, the 9/11 terrorist attacks against the United States also tremendously aided the PRC.[71] Al Qaeda executed the horrific, unprecedented terrorist attacks, intending for the United States to intervene in Afghanistan and for its military to be defeated there, as the Soviets were in their long war. But al Qaeda made a gross miscalculation. US intervention, however imperfect, never involved the level of commitment the Soviets deployed or that the terrorists sought.

However, 9/11 and the Iraq War became windfall victories for the PRC. The attacks distracted the United States from the PRC's expansion by centering its strategic attention on the Middle East. The PRC took full advantage of that preoccupation to rise to great power status with few impediments, and often with the active encouragement of many business partners in the US, to its present position as the peer competitor and main threat to the interests and position of the United States.

The PRC's move was premeditated and carefully planned. Within five hours of the 9/11 attacks, Jiang called President Bush to offer China's support and cooperation in fighting terrorism. This began the Sino-American cooperation in the war on terror. Later, Jiang was hailed as a wise man who successfully used the 9/11 attacks to reverse the US attempt to contain the PRC, improving the PRC's international environment and allowing the PRC to seize an invaluable and historically unique strategic opportunity—a period of twenty years to grow its strength while repressing the Uyghur and other Muslim ethnic groups under the guise of the war on terror.[72]

Since 9/11, the US has expended many military and economic resources in its fight in Afghanistan, and later in Iraq and Libya, in the wake of the "Arab Spring," as well as more recently in Syria and Yemen. Washington's focus was devoted to winning the wars under United States Central Command's rubric.

Of course, while it was so occupied, international politics did not stop. This is not a football game. The US does not get to call a "time out" in great power competition. Relative changes in the distribution of power and the correlation of forces continued unabated. The most significant of these was that the PRC grew in power, capabilities, influence, and intentions.

As in the 1990s, Washington's priority was the wars in southwest Asia, not peer competitive threats. The PRC was perhaps a threat on the horizon, and its truculent behavior during the EP-3E incident was alarming and did not augur well for Beijing's intentions, but it was not the US's equal—and most doubted that it would be. A major consequence of 9/11 was that the US did not move to check Beijing's rise and expansion, including into the South China Sea, when it might have done so at lower cost and far more effectively.

US myopia afforded the PRC a rare gift in international politics: to move from a relatively weak great-power position to peer-competitive rival without effective resistance or balancing against it. Washington's strategic nearsightedness permitted the PRC to change the status quo against the interests of the US and its allies, such as Japan, in the East and South China Seas. The United States did not seem to notice that the PRC's economic growth allowed it to establish international economic institutions such as the Asia Infrastructure

Investment Bank (AIIB) and the Belt and Road Initiative (BRI), which laid the foundation for a new economic order.[73] It enabled Beijing to spread its influence in Africa, Central and South Asia, Oceania, the Middle East, Europe, and Latin America. In the military realm, the PRC augmented its conventional and strategic military capabilities, including in cyberspace and space, with the development of hypersonic weapons. Equally important, it professionalized its military and now is preparing it for joint operations against the US and its allies.

Most momentous of all, the period of unchecked expansion allowed the formation of the ruling Xi Jinping clique and the abandonment of the Deng Xiaoping-inspired more cautious approach to international politics. With Xi's rise, the US faces a leader who has a grand strategy of Chinese dominance. Xi is a bold leader, determined to challenge the US, and he is doing so with dispatch.

As a thought experiment, in a world in which 9/11 or Iraq War did not happen, and incidents such as the April 2001 EP-3E incident off Hainan Island provoked a sufficient US response to arrest China's unalloyed growth and expansion, the US could have ensured the PRC's territorial expansion in the East and South China Seas was denied by a powerful US and allied response. The US and the global community might have impressed upon Beijing that it could not achieve its aims through bullying, and it would have to use diplomacy to resolve territorial claims.

Unambiguously, the PRC is the strategic beneficiary of 9/11 and, in its wake, of Washington's strategic decision to invade Iraq. The PRC acted boldly to solidify its impressive rise while the US directed its prime strategic focus elsewhere. The Iraq War cost the US mightily in every respect: those killed, about 4,400, wounded, about 32,000, lives destroyed through suicide, PTSD, divorce, drug abuse, and shattered lives, the estimated $3.5 trillion pecuniary expense, and opportunity cost. Those numbers do not include the US contractors killed and wounded, Iraqis, or US allies. Of course, those costs were not borne equally, but overwhelmingly by working- and middle-class Americans. The legacy of the Iraq War remains on the services and the research and development, as well as procurement choices they made in those years. The focus of the intelligence community and services on Iraq and the counterinsurgency mission provided the PRC with a window of opportunity they exploited but also shaped the intelligence community and services to counterinsurgency missions to the neglect of the prodigious demands of great power competition and high intensity warfare. The legacy of the war is lasting, and its effects remain with the US national security community.

Accordingly, 9/11 and the Iraq War provided the PRC with time to expand its power, develop its capabilities, and train its forces. It had time to undermine the US in global politics and further its influence in capitals around the world. The PRC now is the most formidable peer competitor the US has faced. Whether the PRC defeats the US is the strategically dispositive question of the twenty-first century—but it is long past time that the US recognizes and responds to the challenge to defeat the CCP.

The Obama administration carried the Bush administration's policies as well. Obama had an early test on March 5–12, 2009, with PRC harassment of the USNS *Impeccable* (T-AGOS-23) in the South China Sea. This incident was a more forceful echo of the 2001, 2002, and 2003 *Bowditch* (T-AGS-62) harassments by PLAN and Chinese fishing vessels in the Yellow Sea. Beijing was concerned that another "color revolution" was in the offing after Obama's 2009 Cairo speech. In Obama's address at Cairo university, he stated the US stands with Muslims who are oppressed, which was an unlikely reference to the PRC's oppression in Xinjiang, but it was seen in Beijing as an attack.[74] Second, President Obama referenced that governments must reflect the will of the people, everywhere.[75] The CCP interpreted this as support for a color revolution directed at them. After the Cairo speech, the PRC accelerated the growth of its military capabilities.

In November 2011, President Obama's speech to the Parliament of Australia announced the so-called "pivot" to Asia, later rebranded as the "rebalance to the Pacific," reminded the audience of America's strong, historic commitment to the Asia-Pacific, and pledged his administration's increased attention to the region.[76] In the aftermath of the speech, the PRC again tested US resolve with the April-June 2012 Scarborough Shoal incident between the PRC and the Philippines in the South China Sea.

In April 2012, PRC commercial ships were discovered removing giant clams and coral heads from Scarborough Shoal just 140 nautical miles northwest of Manila and within the Philippines' Exclusive Economic Zone (EEZ). This discovery and the resultant dispatch of nearly a dozen PRC maritime forces from their coast guard and navy instigated a standoff that ultimately intimidated the Philippine coast guard and fishermen away from their ancestral fishing grounds.[77]

Due to the failure of the pro-CCP school of thinking, the US State Department effectively abetted the PRC's occupation of Scarborough Shoal when Kurt Campbell, then the Assistant Secretary of State for East Asian and Pacific Affairs, ostensibly led the negotiation of an agreement for the mutual withdrawal of PLAN and Philippine naval assets from Scarborough. Even as the negotiations were ongoing, the Philippine president traveled to the United States to personally beseech the support of President Obama, he received no specific statements of support, and no operational support followed. Beijing interpreted this as a signal of disinterest and weakness from Obama.[78]

The plan was flawed as evidenced by the PRC reneging on the agreement. It refused to remove its vessels from the shoal upon the agreed date in June 2012. That set a bad precedent, the fruits of which the world witnesses today as the PRC attempts to evict the Philippines from Second Thomas Shoal, also called Ayungin Shoal by the Filipinos and what the PRC terms Ren'ai Reef (*Ren'ai Jiao*). The Philippines has a vessel, BRP *Sierra Madre*, a former US Navy LST (Landing Ship, Tank), grounded there since 1999. On August 5, 2023, the Chinese Coast Guard fired a water cannon at two Philippine resupply vessels to prevent their resupply mission.[79] This was in direct violation of the November 2002 Declaration on the Conduct of Parties in the South China Sea between ASEAN (Association of Southeast Asian Nations) and the PRC.

Once again in 2023, Beijing is testing the Biden administration to see if it will support its Filipino ally with whom the US has a Mutual Defense Treaty.[80] For US national security, losing the South China Sea means losing Taiwan, support of key allies like the Philippines, partners like Vietnam, and losing support of the critical ally Japan that depends upon maritime access through the South China Sea.

The Scarborough Shoal incident was a watershed event in PRC's expansionist strategy as the Obama administration failed this test of strategic leadership. The PRC had established itself as the sole naval power at the shoal, formerly the sovereign territory of the Republic of the Philippines. The PRC's maritime forces seized the sovereign rights from a US treaty ally—something never done before—without firing a shot.

The ramifications of the Scarborough Shoal incident were not just confined to the waters of the South China Sea. For instance, it is worth noting that the leader of the CCP Leading Group on maritime affairs that orchestrated the seizure was at that time not well known in the West, a man named Xi Jinping, who had been selected to become CCP's next General Secretary, and thus dictator of the PRC, the following year.

Beijing soon realized that there would be no danger from the Obama administration and that the PRC could continue its expansion in the South China Sea. Soon thereafter, in early 2013, the world began to witness the PRC's building of seven artificial islands in the Spratly Islands.[81] Three of the islands each contain a 10,000-foot runway capable of supporting PLA air force bombers, reconnaissance and fighter aircraft, and enough pier space for any of the PLAN's aircraft carriers or large-deck amphibious ships. Despite assurances from Xi to Obama in 2014 that the PRC would not militarize the islands, today these are fully militarized bases, three of which are the size and capacity of Pearl Harbor.

The failure of engagement has had tangible impact on the balance of power in Asia. The PLA now has seven military installations in the South China Sea, over 600 nautical miles from the mainland, that provide the PRC assurance that they have effectively secured sovereignty over the South China Sea. Today the PRC's warships, submarines and aircraft are deployed to the South China Sea at a conservative ratio of 10 to 1 compared to the United States.

Moreover, the Obama Administration did not aggressively support the 2016 ruling against the PRC by the Permanent Court of Arbitration (PCA) regarding the case brought by the Republic of the Philippines that challenged the so-called "Nine Dashed Line" that assert's Beijing's sovereignty over the South China Sea.

In addition to providing Xi Jinping inspiration for pursuing a decade of a maritime sovereignty campaign inside the First Island Chain, these events had the negative consequence of providing then Philippine President Duterte with justification for siding with the PRC after he came to office in 2016, something that is only now being redressed by Philippine President Marcos. The strategic impact being that Beijing was once again given time to achieve its goal of control over the South China Sea.

Consequently, the overarching failure to secure America's national security interests in the Spratly Islands and Scarborough Shoal disputes was driven by the Obama administrations *de facto* policy of "not provoking the PRC." According to a former senior naval officer: "The Obama administration was very clear that they did not want to do anything to provoke the PRC . . . that was an unwritten policy."[82] The lack of an effective response to the Scarborough Shoal incident in 2012, the building of bases in the Spratly Islands between 2013–2015, and the failure to reinforce the Republic of the Philippines in 2016 by word and deed were all unfortunate and disastrous choices by the Obama administration's unwritten policy of "not provoking Beijing." Just as importantly, the failure to support a treaty ally severely damaged US credibility, not only with the Philippines, but across the entire Indo-Pacific region.

Only with the Trump administration was there the start of effective resistance. Secretary of State Mike Pompeo's address at the Nixon Library in July 2020 explicitly broke with engagement policies.[83] He asked the following obvious questions that had previously not been asked publicly by any other American administration, although some of which had been hotly debated during the Cold War, especially during the Reagan administration: First, what do the American people have to show now fifty years on from engagement with China? Second, did the theories of our leaders that proposed a Chinese evolution toward freedom and democracy prove to be true? Third, is this China's definition of a win-win situation? Fourth, is America safer? And fifth, do we have a greater likelihood of peace for ourselves and peace for the generations which will follow us?

The former secretary answered these questions with the following, unprecedented, answer: "We must admit a hard truth that should guide us in the years and decades to come, that if we want to have a free twenty-first century, and not the Chinese century of which Xi Jinping dreams, the old paradigm of blind engagement with China simply won't get it done. We must not continue it and we must not return to it."[84]

This speech, combined with the earlier release from 2018 of key national security documents such as the *National Security Strategy of the United States* (NSS) for the first time identified the PRC as the greatest threat to US national security.[85] For the American people, the PRC-generated Covid pandemic accelerated the recognition of the PRC threat. Some of the Trump administration's policies were continued by President Biden; many more were reversed. But most importantly, the emphasis and tone of the Biden administration marked a return to the old regime. It was back to the pro-CCP school of thought regarding how the relationship with the PRC should be defined by the US.[86]

Deng Xiaoping's Political Warfare Strategy of Threat Deflation

Deng was masterful at his political warfare strategy of threat deflation. Through his strategy, he maximized the PRC's chances of, first, not generating a balancing coalition to oppose the PRC's rise, and second, removed any US consideration of regime change against the CCP. This was a remarkable feat of statesmanship that occurred in plain sight. Thus, in the pantheon of strategists, Deng should rank as German Chancellor Otto von Bismarck's equal. Both were master threat deflators, and thus accomplished what was supremely difficult—to expand their state's power rapidly without generating a coalition of balancing powers to resist their rise. Germany would not be balanced until the first decade of the twentieth century and then only because of supremely costly strategic missteps by Kaiser Wilhelm II. While the PRC's rise may be dated approximately to 1992, it has yet to encounter sufficient balancing.

In the wake of the Tiananmen Square Massacre, Deng recognized the CCP's vulnerability. Immediately he stressed economic reform and development while continuing to crack down on dissent and to remove Western influence. In doing so, he was able to minimize the West's reaction and prevent the West from overthrowing the CCP and advancing the cause of Chinese democracy in its place. Deng's rapid actions were cunning statesmanship.

They kept the CCP in power and laid the foundation for China's tremendous growth in power to the point where it is now a rival to the US. That China could be a peer of the US would have been unthinkable to American foreign policy experts in 1989 and reveals Deng's strategic genius to chart that course by cracking down in the immediate aftermath, while soon thereafter, enlisting Wall Street and US business interests as his allies.

Deng provided a masterclass in *Realpolitik*. The PRC was weak and confronted a precarious strategic situation. With the conclusion of the Cold War and thus the absence of the Soviet threat, and Tiananmen Square, the PRC was vulnerable to US pressure for significant political reform of the CCP, including pressure to democratize. Beijing needed favorable conditions for its economic development. Accordingly, a confrontational approach was not an option. China was not yet a great power, so it had to avoid being a target while Deng laid the foundation for a challenge to the United States.[87] This threat deflation strategy contributed to the US's inability to identify the PRC as the peer competitive threat as it is now.

In a series of talks with the CCP leaders, Deng instructed them to "keep calm, handle well our own affairs, and do not stick our head out." In April 1992, when he talked with his staff about China's development issues and the appropriate political warfare strategy, he first used the now famous phrase of "hide one's capabilities and bide one's time (韬光养晦)." This was the genesis of Deng's "24-Character Strategy," "韬光养晦," which is usually summarized in English as "hide our capabilities and bide our time." Deng wanted the CCP to maintain a low profile and hide its real intentions, as he said: "We must hide our capabilities and bide our time to work hard for a few more years, only then can we become a real greater political power, and only after that, China's voice will carry very different weight in the international community."

Deng's talks were later synthesized into the "28-Character Strategy" to guide the PRC's foreign relations: "Calmly observe, stabilize our own position, quietly handle affairs, hide our intension, be good at pretending to be clumsy, never stick our head out, and achieve more" (冷静观察、稳住阵脚、沉着应付、韬光养晦、善于守拙、决不当头、有所作为).

The CCP's behavior post-Mao and pre-Xi can be seen as the "period of strategic opportunity" provided by the US. While avoiding military entanglements in the region and, especially, with the United States, the PRC eagerly pursued—free from any serious challenger—the political and economic opportunities available to a rising power, particularly increasing its comprehensive national strength and international competitiveness.[88]

As Deng recognized, the CCP faced considerable peril if they could not penetrate the Western economic ecosystem. Economic growth would strengthen their power, provide the technology and knowledge to defeat the US, and would weaken popular resistance to the CCP's rule and aid the CCP's claim to political legitimacy. The PRC did so successfully by using the promise of the China market to Western firms in return for the transfer of Western knowledge, wealth, investment, technology, and procedures.[89]

Deng's political warfare strategy was a great success and was sustained by his successors. In a typical speech, Hu Jintao told an international conference that "China will firmly adhere to the road of peaceful development."[90] PRC officials consistently repeated that the PRC was on a "peaceful rise" to what exactly—hegemony or preponderance, the end state was always deliberately vague.

Importantly, as we have argued, the PRC did not accomplish this tremendous growth alone. The West truly made this possible. The PRC's rise was made possible because the US allowed it to enter the world's free-trade system. The PRC has flourished precisely because it entered the West's economic ecosystem a generation ago. For decades, the PRC has used this ecosystem to grow rapidly.

For more than thirty years, the PRC has gained through legal and illegal means an astronomical $4.4 trillion from the United States.[91] Additionally, the US has lost $200 billion to $600 billion annually because of the PRC's theft, and the US has lost several million good-paying manufacturing jobs. The PRC achieved economic success in large measure by taking advantage of the working classes in both the PRC and the United States. The Chinese working classes continue to pay a high price for the regime's ambition: wages are artificially low, and labor conditions rival anything as bad as any in Great Britain or Europe in the nineteenth century. Once workers leave factories, they encounter other dangers for their health from chronic air and water pollution in Chinese cities. A consequence of the PRC entering the West's ecosystem has been to weaken the West's manufacturing power and introduce dependency on China's products.

The US helped to create its most powerful enemy by giving the PRC access to talent, markets, capital, technologies, and higher education systems. This permitted the PRC to build its economic might, which, in turn, allowed it to create a formidable military with an increasing capability to project its power globally. As argued, the PRC's leadership was shaken to its core by the Tiananmen Square massacre and, more significantly, by the collapse of the Soviet Union.

The CCP feared it might be next, and as US policy began to shift in the early 1990s, and in the wake of the First Iraq War, the CCP wondered if they were targeted. As Stewart Paterson argues in his exceptional analysis of the PRC's economic growth: "The collapse of the Soviet Union demonstrated the potential political price of economic failure. . . . China was keen to learn the lessons of Russian failure."[92] The foremost of these lessons was that "isolation from technological progress that Western societies were making almost guaranteed subordination in the world order. . . . [China] desperately needed know-how and skills, and this was only likely to come from abroad if it was tied into a rules-based trade system, which meant WTO [World Trade Organization] membership."[93] Not being a member hindered "technology transfer and foreign direct investment (FDI), which, in turn, was preventing China from taking, as [the Chinese leadership] saw it, its rightful place in the world . . . and [the CCP's] ability to deliver better living standards to the population."[94]

Even before the PRC entered the WTO in 2001, it prioritized export-oriented growth, the reform of state-owned enterprises, and FDI, which provided a foundation for its economic miracle beginning in the 1990s. FDI flowed into the PRC from multinational companies and, according to Paterson, when combined with the "knock-on effects of this investment, were the major drivers of Chinese productivity improvement and hence economic growth."[95]

The US supported the PRC's economic growth and membership in the WTO, facilitating both with the expectation that they would be beneficial for the US economy and that the integration of the PRC into the Western economic ecosystem would compel China to democratize. This was a colossal blunder based on the hubris and ignorance of Western political leaders that existed from the 1990s until Donald Trump's presidency.

Predictions that the PRC was on the wrong side of a Hegelian conception of history are painful reminders that, in reality, Hegelian arguments cannot cause their preferred historical outcome. Instead of forcing its democratization, China's economic growth fueled the CCP's agenda of the Great Rejuvenation, which has become increasingly aggressive and globally ambitious. Economic prosperity legitimized China's flawed political system and made it possible for a dictator such as Xi to sustain his control.

The US and European Union (EU) lost any hope of compelling change when both supported investment, trade, and WTO membership for the PRC without linking these "carrots" to the "stick" of political reform and respect for human rights.[96] As discussed above, and as Mann summarizes, "In 1994, after President Clinton abandoned his attempt to use trade as a lever for improving human rights in China, he and his administration needed to divert attention from this embarrassing reversal." They did not want "to concede that they had just downgraded the cause of human rights," preferring instead to emphasize the integration of the PRC into Western political principles and norms.[97] The consequence, Mann submits, was that "integration became, above all, the justification for unrestricted trade with China" and compelled the question, which the West no longer can answer with confidence: "Who's integrating whom?"[98]

In truth, the West never insisted upon such measures as capital account convertibility and a floating exchange rate, which would have allowed adjustments, particularly in the financial system, to occur at the expense of the CCP's control of the economy. The PRC's neo-mercantilist economic model was allowed to survive: The West placed too much faith in the PRC's willingness to play by the rule book and reform its political system and did too little to compel compliance.[99] As a result, the world confronts the consequences of this choice to not require the PRC to reform.

In sum, reflecting upon these successive US presidential administrations, it becomes clear that the actions of the Trump presidency led to the end of decades of threat deflation. Under Trump's administration, the PRC was identified as a peer threat and measures advanced, even if incompletely, to formulate a strategy of victory, reduce US vulnerabilities, rollback PRC gains, and further broader competitive strategies to confront the PRC.

The Biden administration has rhetorically expressed some measure of confrontation from time to time while advancing neo-engagement in principle, if not as an explicit policy. Biden's creation of a "China House," the Office of China Coordination, in the Department of State has the possibility of being a positive step forward for addressing the PRC threat. It is tasked with providing information regarding the PRC threat and accelerating and coordinating the government's reaction to it. Earlier, the CIA created the "China Mission Center" to aid the Intelligence Community direct resources, funding, and personnel to counter Beijing's expanding diplomatic, technological, and military power.

These actions are long overdue. Collectively, they indicate that the flame of strategic thought is not completely extinguished in Washington. Sadly, for decades it was. Wall Street, Silicon Valley, and the United States government supported China's economic growth in the disastrous belief that a wealthier, more prosperous China would be more democratic and peaceful, becoming a "responsible stakeholder" in the liberal international order.

The camarilla of the pro-CCP school held profoundly mistaken, naïve, and misguided assumptions regarding the behavior of the CCP. Lamentably, it was completely divorced from an understanding of the motivations and strategic objectives of the CCP, a strategic conception of US national interests, and an understanding of importance of the relative distribution of power within the correlation of forces necessary for securing the US position as the world's dominant military power.

The consequence was as the PRC became richer it siphoned off a substantial and consistent percentage of this new wealth to increase its military might, technological prowess, and diplomatic influence. In addition, this new paradigm yielded a US economy that was dependent upon the PRC for critical manufacturing and goods, including pharmaceuticals, personal protective equipment, and antibiotics. Today the PRC is more prosperous, more bellicose, and more determined to supplant the liberal order and the US position in the world.

Yet, in the face of Beijing's rise, the pro-CCP school remains robust on Wall Street, Silicon Valley, government, think tanks, media, and academe. Recently, given the backlash against the pro-CCP school that arose during the Trump Administration, the strategic messaging shifted to appeals for just the right amount of technological decoupling from China. These calls have been labeled by some, most notably in the European Union, as "de-risking" and are profoundly misguided. This is in the wake of the October 2022 announcement by the Biden administration that it was imposing export controls on advanced semiconductors and chip-making equipment to weaken China's semiconductor and AI development. In December 2022, Biden placed thirty-six Chinese groups, most notably Yangtze Memory Technologies Corporation (YMTC), on the "entities list" to hinder the ability of US firms to export critical technologies to them, and twenty-one Chinese firms were listed as "foreign direct product rule," which means non-American companies are prohibited from exporting items with US technological content.

There are three flaws of any effort to find a "Goldilocks amount" regarding high-tech trade and technology transfer to the PRC. First, even to consider trade with the CCP is to lack an understanding of the odious nature of the regime. The CCP is uniquely vicious government that has killed tens of millions of Chinese citizens, perpetually violates human rights and presently is committing a genocide of Muslims in Xinjiang, lied about the origins of the Covid-19 pandemic and thus facilitated its spread, and ruthlessly exploits people and the environment.

Most importantly, in 2019 the CCP formally declared "People's War" against the US, explicitly indicating that it is the enemy of US and intends to defeat the US and its allies.[100] An understanding of the character of the CCP should compel anyone concerned with human rights to terminate any connection with it and the entities it controls. As the CCP is at war with the US, the US is compelled to respond accordingly. In turn, this requires Wall Street, Silicon Valley, and all US entities to decide whether they will assist the US or the CCP to answer the fundamental issue of the twenty-first century—will this century be defined by the liberal international order or by the repression of the CCP?

Second, understanding the PRC threat requires a change in mindset—we need to think like strategists rather than financiers. With the defeat of the

Soviet Union, the ideas, practices, understanding, and training necessary for peer competition—most importantly not only how to defeat a peer competitor but how to prevent one from rising—were supplanted by the doyens of finance and foreign investment.

A fundamental rule of strategy is obvious but rather painfully it must be expressed because the US did it: do not fund your enemy. It is a shameful fact that Western firms pursued investments in the PRC, technology, and knowledge transfer to Beijing, and permitted Chinese entities to raise funds on US capital markets, including those with known or suspected ties to the People's Liberation Army, to those directly and indirectly linked to the Muslim genocide, and to the CCP. The last is by definition since every Chinese entity needs the CCP's permission to exist.

The US must possess an understanding of the relative distribution of power. As ever more investment, technology, and knowledge entered the PRC year after year, the US grew relatively weaker as its wealth flowed into the PRC rather than to investments within the US or friendly states. The CCP was strengthened, and any hope for its liberalization or overthrow was lost. Trade with the PRC in any advanced technology is helping Beijing dominate the commanding heights of semiconductors and AI, which weakens the US military, economy, and technological leadership, and in time will cost the US its superiority.

Trade in high tech with the PRC is supremely foolish because of how it assists the relative power of the PRC to the cost of the US and due to the risks any US entity incurs cooperating with a Chinese entity. In 2020, the Department of Homeland Security (DHS) released a significant advisory to US businesses warning of the risks associated with trade with Chinese entities. The advisory noted the persistent and increasing risk of Chinese government-sponsored data theft due to newly enacted PRC laws.[101] As of July 2023, the laws included the PRC's 2023 Counter-Espionage Law Update, the 2021 Cyber Vulnerability Reporting Law, the 2021 Personal Information Protection Law, the 2021 Anti-Foreign Sanctions Law, the 2021 Data Security Law, the 2017 National Intelligence Law, the 2017 Cybersecurity Law, and the 2015 National Security Law.[102] These laws compel PRC businesses and citizens—including through academic institutions, research service providers, and investors—to support and facilitate the PRC's government access to the collection, transmission, and storage of data. In sum, they compel Chinese entities to permit spying by the PRC's intelligence services.

As a result, foreign firms trading with the PRC run a perpetual risk of state-sponsored data theft that accelerates the reduction of foreign competitors' domestic market share. It also hastens China's acquisition of technological dominance in critical markets that have long been led by US, Japanese, and European firms—including in aerospace, semiconductors, robotics, artificial intelligence systems, biometrics, cyber intelligence, genomics, pharmaceutical medicines, and sustainable/green energy materials.

From a strategic perspective, there is no "Goldilocks" amount of safe trade in high tech with China. Indeed, the right amount is zero. As the Biden's administration "China House" and trade restrictions demonstrate, strategy—not finance—needs to govern US relations with the CCP. This recognition requires ending trade in any good or service—well beyond high tech—that advances the PRC's relative power in relation to the US.

CHAPTER THREE

IMPLICATIONS FOR THE UNITED STATES

"I have noticed too much of a tendency towards what might be called Next-War-itis—the propensity of much of the defense establishment to be in favor of what might be needed in a future conflict."
—Robert M. Gates, Secretary of Defense, May 2008[1]

It did not have to be this way. The US did not have to confront an enemy as formidable as the PRC. A second Cold War is evidence of a profound failure by US leaders. The profound costs, risks, and sacrifices of this new Cold War are not going to be borne solely by the elite who caused this disastrous condition but will be by the American people and by US allies.

US power was unrivaled at the conclusion of the Cold War. What the succeeding generation of strategists had to do was sustain what their predecessors had given them: economic, ideological, and military supremacy, and an international order that the US led, and which favored it. Russia was broken. China was poor, and its military only a threat to its neighbors like India and Vietnam. The abundance of allies would have included all the centers of economic might, the EU, Japan, and the Republic of Korea. Saudi Arabia and the Gulf sheikdoms would have looked to the US for their safety. The security of the United States and its allies would have been preeminent. Indeed, it would have been the most secure the country ever had been. Had they followed the principles of strategy they would have aborted the PRC's rise and likely placed the CCP under such stress that it would be focused internally, or fractured, or overthrown. The unipolar moment would have become a unipolar half-century or more. The Chinese people would have been freed from the yoke of the CCP. The rest of the world would have been liberated from the CCP's exploitation of people and environment.

Those who caused the US victory in World War II and the Cold War, the strategic predecessors of those post-Cold War strategists, provided the right institutional structure and willingness to embrace victory over the foe. For example, the Strategic Air Command (SAC) of the United States Air Force was one of the most powerful tools to deter Soviet aggression. Its capabilities and high standards for its airmen ensured that SAC would always be ready to attack the Soviet Union, which guaranteed the credibility of the US nuclear deterrent. The US Army faced the great stresses of Korea, Vietnam, and the creation of the All-Volunteer Force but addressed its problems to provide a conventional, tactical, and theater deterrent of aggression by the Soviet Union, its Warsaw Pact allies, and North Korea for Washington's NATO allies, key allies and partners in the Middle East, and Japan and South Korea. US Navy Secretary John Lehman advanced the Maritime Strategy to deploy the US Navy in a manner to threaten the flanks of the Soviet Union.[2] This contributed to NATO's conventional deterrent of Warsaw Pact aggression and ensured that the war would only be fought in Europe. The Maritime Strategy also increased the ability of the Navy to hold at risk Soviet nuclear ballistic missile submarines that were attempting to use the Arctic ice sheet as a bastion to attack the US and its allies.

That was the remarkable history of US military accomplishments to deter the country's enemies. What we have today is a very different situation. The post-Cold War elite not only failed to prevent the PRC's rise but—in a historically unique case of strategic idiocy—contributed to it. This chapter presents the major findings of the study for senior United States national security decision-makers and the American people drawn from the arguments of the book. There are nine significant implications of the study's identification of the causes and consequences of threat deflation and thus why the US underestimated the PRC threat for many decades in the wake of the Cold War. These are organized in three categories. First, those relevant to power politics and the principles of strategy. Second, we provide an analysis of what the US IC and military did that contributed to failure. Third, we consider what the PRC accomplished to threat deflate successfully.

Regarding power politics and the principles of strategy, we consider, first, the fundamental importance of power politics concepts for framing threats to US national security, and policy responses that must be comprehended by senior civilian and military national security decision-makers. Understanding power politics permits realistic assumptions about the future of the Sino-American relationship and Washington's relationship with other great powers. The change in the distribution of power to the great favor of Washington had a dramatic effect of lowering America's guard. The US national security community became vulnerable to threat deflation, weakened its ability to evaluate great power threats, and had a profoundly difficult time adjusting to the new distribution of power with the PRC's rise.

Second, the US national security community must support the education of strategists so that younger generations may possess the knowledge they need in the fight against PRC. Education in the principles of power politics is essential so that strategists have the intellectual firepower to identify what must be accomplished to achieve victory in the fight against the CCP.

Third, understanding of the ideology of Communism and thus why the PRC had the intention to attack and defeat the US is essential. The CCP's ideology explains its motivation to fight the US until the US is defeated. It will not moderate through engagement or compromise, and it will never become democratic. Equally, understanding the CCP's ideology explains why the CCP is illegitimate and possesses profound weaknesses.

Fourth, the absence of presidential leadership in the post-Cold War period has hindered the ability of national security decision-makers to formulate a strategy to defeat the CCP threat. The interests of US business and Wall Street, among others, which furthered engagement with the PRC predominated as did 9/11 and its consequences. Many of the problems identified in this study might have been resolved if there had been adequate presidential leadership.

Next, we analyze what the US IC and military did. The first issue is the failure of the US intelligence community to identify the PRC as an existential threat, which greatly weakened the ability of national security decision-makers to identify and act against the threat. The fundamental assumptions regarding the CCP and the PRC's behavior seem to have been informed by the pro-CCP school of thought. Ultimately, the IC was aiding threat deflation, and hindering the obligatory and forceful response to the PRC's expansion. The IC never seems to have conducted analyses of the CCP and PRC's grand strategy and intentions through the lens of power politics. Unhappy truths regarding the nature of the enemy and horribly, perhaps fatally, misguided US policies are always unpleasant to deliver to senior national security decision-makers, but they were in the Cold War and should have been in this equally important instance too.

Second, as a result of the IC's near pathologic commitment to threat deflation, American military leaders failed to safeguard America's military power, which they had inherited from the massive buildup during WWII and strategic forethought throughout the Cold War. Given the atrocities at Tiananmen in 1989, concerns expressed by junior officers about what amounted to as an "open door" policy granting PLA counterparts access to various US military ships and facilities, to the small minority within the IC that warned of the PRC's strategic intentions, America's senior uniformed officer corps, starting in the early 1990s, did not take these warnings seriously. Worse yet is that they adopted the ideology of "engagement" and provided the PLA with the very knowledge that they in turn used to help conduct the biggest military build-up since WWII.

Third, as the epigram at the beginning of this chapter from US Defense Secretary Robert Gates captures, the minor war today in Afghanistan or Iraq was always more important than the major war with the PRC later. The necessity of fighting wars against terrorists and insurgents heavily occupied US national security decision-makers. The result was the peer competitive threat of the PRC grew without effective opposition and the US position in Afghanistan and Iraq was lost as well.

Fourth, the lack of examination of assumptions was pernicious in the decades of threat deflation. This included, first, that history was at its end, and great power threats were an artifact of the past and therefore cooperation with Russia or the PRC was benign from the perspective of US national security. Second, there was a bias that the US possesses the assumption of time to address future problems and existential threats to itself. The third assumption was that the PRC would be positively transformed through the coterie of engagement policies.

Finally, we consider what the PRC accomplished. It was a testament to the success of Deng's strategy of threat deflation that the PRC's influence was able to penetrate the financial interests of US firms, media, think tanks, and of individuals, including politicians. The problem of elite capture, where far too many US politicians and officials, in addition to business, financiers, media, academics, think tanks, and foundations, were profiting from the PRC's rise. Thus, these parties had an interest in threat deflation and shaping analyses that favored engagement and cooperative policies. Unfortunately, this is a situation that continues to this day and that must be reversed immediately.

Power Politics and the Principles of Strategy

This section analyzes the failure of the US national security community to adhere to and teach power politics and the principles of strategy. These essential tools are still not guiding decision-making and not being taught to younger generations, and so the major implication is that the US still lacks the right intellectual framework for understanding the PRC threat and formulating the necessary domestic and international responses. US national security decision-makers rightfully consult those with expertise on China's history, civilization, and culture. But they do not consult those with a grounding in power politics and great power behavior. They should. The PRC's behavior is defined by power politics. Its actions are far closer to a traditional great power than dynastic China. Power politics and an understanding of Communism should be at the fore for understanding why Beijing acts as it does.

Failure of Civilian and Military Leadership to View National Security Policy Through the Lens of Power Politics and the Principles of Strategy

A fundamental problem identified in this study is a lack of understanding of why the logic of power politics must be applied to US national security policy in all circumstances related to a potential peer competitor. The lack of this intellectual discipline led to the triumph of "End of History" idealistic reasoning. It influenced decades of professional military education, strategic analysts, commentators, and national security decision-makers, and so contributed to the threat deflation problem. Throughout history, the principles of power politics define great power relationships. They should be taught to decision-makers and analysts. They should govern national security policy and the relationship that the US has with other states.

Marcus Porcius Cato (the Elder, 234 BC–149 BC) always ended his speeches in the Roman Senate—no matter the topic—with the recognition that Rome's peer competitor, Carthage, must be destroyed (*Carthago delenda est*). Carthage was finally vanquished after the end of the Third Punic War in 146 BC, three years after Cato's death. His focus on the peer competitive threat perpetually reminded Roman leaders of the danger to their primacy and of Carthage's determination to defeat them. Today, Cato's clear and powerful insight concerning the necessity of focusing upon peer competitive threats must be institutionalized in the US Department of Defense.

The fundamental interests of the United States are to preserve its position in international politics as the world's dominant state. The US must ensure that its leadership is maintained against potential peer competitors. It failed to accomplish this in the wake of the Cold War. The principles of strategy, which have been traditionally employed to explain the rise and decline of states, are essential for civilian and military leadership to understand and to apply to national security policies. US national security decision-makers must view the world through the lens of these principles to advance the US national interest. With the return of great power competition, US national security decision-makers must focus on the three principles of strategy.

The first of these is the recognition that power is the coin of realm in great power competition. US defense policy must be anchored on the understanding that the most significant instrument in international politics is power. For most states, including China, India, and the US, power equals the total of its military, economic, diplomatic capabilities and effectiveness, population size, geographic position, technological prowess and adaptability, and natural resources. In essence, the amount of power a state possesses pivots around three considerations: the number of people who can work and fight; their economic productivity and innovative capacity; and the effectiveness of the political system in exacting and pooling individual contributions to advance national interests.

Population is an essential component but alone cannot confer power, as is clearly demonstrated by the relative weakness of Bangladesh, Indonesia, or Brazil. To be truly powerful, the economy, the source of military power, must be efficient and innovative. Of course, those advantages cannot be realized without political effectiveness, the ability of governments to extract resources to advance national goals and the willpower to continue in the face of political or economic adversity or military setbacks or failures. Politically effective governments garner relatively more resources and have greater determination and are then able to expand national power. The unhappy experience of the US in Vietnam is important to keep in mind. North Vietnam defeated a more populous and affluent South Vietnam—despite massive assistance from the United States and its allies to Saigon—due to its ruthless extraction of resources, willpower, and aid from key allies like the Soviet Union and the PRC.

The number and wealth of allies is also important. This is because allies often augment the dominant state's power through their military effectiveness, intelligence community, economic might, and natural resources. Of course, allies may also introduce problems for the dominant state, including manipulating the hegemon's power to advance the ally's interests. However, on the whole, allies are assets that strengthen and deepen a hegemon's capabilities.

To this understanding of the components of power, Harvard political scientist Joseph Nye's description of the importance of soft power—getting others to want what you want—is a significant contribution.[3] Nye contrasted "soft power" with "hard power," the military, economic, diplomatic, and technological capabilities of a state. Stalin's famous quip, "How many divisions has the Pope?" was intended to mock the power of the Catholic Church. But history turned his remark on its head. The Pope could not evict the Red Army from Poland in 1945, but Pope John Paul II's role in undermining Communist rule in that country in the late 1970s and 1980s underscores the importance of soft power. Indeed, Beijing has well learned this significance. Its establishment of Confucius Institutes, cultural centers promoting Chinese philosophy, language, and culture worldwide, while undermining the position of Western philosophy, culture, and languages, is a powerful illustration of Chinese soft power.[4]

At the same time, soft power plays a secondary role and is no substitute for hard power. This is because soft power, in the context of the present Sino-American confrontation, is always difficult to discern or to measure. Moreover, it always occurs within the context of material power. In the present struggle, the capabilities of the PRC and the United States will determine the result of the confrontation.

The second principle for strategy is the distinction between absolute and relative power. While the absolute power that a state has is significant, what is more important is the relative power of the state—how it ranks in terms of power against the power of other states. The example of Great Britain underscores this point. In absolute terms, Great Britain is far more powerful than it was a hundred years ago. However, in relative terms, Great Britain is much weaker than it was then. The rise of Germany, Japan, the Soviet Union/Russia, and the United States mean that Britain is weaker in comparison. London has much less influence than it had a century ago when it ruled the waves, and its empire was arguably the world's greatest military power.

Dominant great powers that do not carefully consider and evaluate the relative distribution of power are condemned to lose their dominance. Thus, how relative power is distributed in international politics is of central importance. Accordingly, trade must be considered with respect to its strategic impact. The free market economists' emphasis on absolute gains from trade must be supplanted by the strategists' emphasis on the distribution of relative power: which state will gain more power from economic exchange must be the metric. Unfortunately, the US did not follow this strategic principle in its relations with the PRC over the last generation.

The central interest of the United States is to remain the world's dominant power. The United States can remain dominant due to its relative power advantages anchored on its impressive military, economic, technological, and soft power capabilities. Moreover, the US should be dominant because this is the best strategy to advance and protect its interests and those of its allies.

The third principle is that US dominance is necessary. Ensuring US primacy takes as its starting point the protection of the US homeland and global interests. These interests include ensuring that critical resources like rare-earth minerals or energy flow to the US and US allies, that the global liberal trade and monetary regimes flourish, that the US dollar remains the global reserve currency, that Washington's worldwide network of allies are reassured and protected, and that peer competitive threats are prevented from rising. If they are not, then the US must apply all its power to defeat the peer. Primacy requires laboring to dissuade potential peer competitors or great powers from challenging the US for hegemony. If enemies need to be fought, primacy allows the enemy to be engaged overseas, away from American soil.

The hallmarks of the current liberal international order—free trade, a robust monetary regime with the US dollar preeminent, increasing respect for human rights—are directly linked to US power. One of history's most significant lessons is that appalling events happen when international orders collapse. The Dark Ages followed Rome's collapse. Hitler succeeded the order established at Versailles. Without US power, the liberal order created by the US will end just as assuredly. Consequently, it is important to acknowledge the six benefits of primacy for the United States.

The first is the most essential for the US. Its primacy ensures the security of the US and its allies because Washington possesses the power to dissuade potential challengers and to coerce, deter, or defeat its enemies. Even with China's rise, a remarkable fact about international politics today is that countries want to align themselves with the United States. Of course, in most cases this is not out of any sense of altruism but because doing so allows them to use the power of the United States for their own purposes—their own protection, or to gain greater influence.

Although US alliances are being tested by the PRC's rise, of approximately 194 countries in the world, about 80 are allied with the US. Their security is tied to the United States through treaties and other formal as well as informal arrangements—and they include almost all of the major economic and military powers. That is a ratio of almost 17 to 1 (84 to 5), and a major change from the Cold War when the ratio was about 1.8 to 1 of states aligned with the United States versus the Soviet Union at the height of the Cold War. Never in

its history has this country, or any country, had so many allies. US primacy—
and the bandwagoning effect it causes as states seek to align with the US—has
also given us extensive influence in international politics, allowing the United
States to shape the behavior of states and international institutions.

A small number of countries are overtly opposed to the United States: the
PRC, Cuba, Iran, North Korea, Venezuela, and now Russia. Only these states
may be expected to consistently resist the interest of the United States. China
is clearly the most important of these states because it is a superpower. The
other states are far weaker than China. For three of these cases, Cuba, Iran,
and Venezuela, it is an anti-US regime that is the source of the problem; the
country itself is not intrinsically anti-American. Indeed, a change of regime in
Havana, Tehran, or Caracas, and even Pyongyang and dare we say it, Beijing,
could very well reorient relations so that they are in greater accord with US
interests. Russia is a more difficult case. Lukewarm relations under Trump
have been replaced by hostility due to Moscow's invasion of Kyiv. Beijing is a
threat to Moscow just as Washington is, and were the Russo-Ukrainian war
to end, there might be an entente with the US due to the PRC's expansionist
drive.

The second benefit of US primacy has been a more peaceful world.
Throughout history, peace and stability have been great benefits of an era
where there was a dominant power—Rome, Britain, or the United States
today. Historians since Edward Gibbon have long recognized the irenic effect
of hegemonic power. US hegemony prevents escalation of disputes among
US allies, such as Japan and South Korea. During the Cold War, US leadership reduced friction among many states that were historical antagonists,
most notably France and West Germany. Today, American primacy helps keep
several complicated relationships aligned—between Greece and Turkey, Israel
and Egypt, India and Pakistan, Indonesia and Australia, and North and South
Korea. This is not to argue that US hegemony fulfills Woodrow Wilson's
vision of ending all war. Wars still occur, as Ukraine sadly illustrates, particularly where Washington's interests are not present, but US power does reduce
war's likelihood—particularly war's worst form—hegemonic wars. As the US
has allowed its relative power to wane, Washington once again confronts this
danger.

Third, US primacy provides the United States the ability to spread elements of its liberal ideology, including democracy. Doing so is positive for the countries concerned as well as the United States because liberal democracies are more likely to align with the US and be sympathetic to the American worldview. Thus, spreading democracy helps maintain US primacy. In addition, once states are governed democratically, the likelihood of any type of conflict is significantly reduced. This is not because democracies do not have clashing interests. Indeed, they do. Rather, it is because they are more open, more transparent, more likely to want to resolve things amicably in concurrence with US leadership. In general, democratic states are good for their citizens as well as for advancing the interests of the US.

Fourth, along with the growth in the number of democratic states around the world has been the growth of the global economy and creation of global "rules of the road." With its allies, the United States created global liberal monetary and trade regimes characterized by free trade and commerce, respect for international property rights, and the mobility of capital. The economic stability and prosperity that stems from this economic order is under threat from the PRC. Indeed, the creation of this order accelerated the PRC's power, and thus its ability to confront the US. In essence, because the US did not prioritize strategy over economics, it faces the PRC threat. Learning from that costly mistake, the US must emphasize its relative economic growth vis-à-vis its rivals. The liberal economic order must be refocused to ensure US relative economic gains are maximized, that US industries are competitive, but equally that essential industries are protected, and US strategic interests are foremost for decision-makers.

Fifth, at present, US primacy permits the US to command the "global commons"—the oceans, the world's airspace, outer space, and even cyber space—allowing the United States to project its power far from its borders, while denying or truncating those common avenues to its enemies. Consequently, the costs of power projection for the United States and its allies are reduced, and the robustness of the United States' conventional and strategic deterrent capabilities is increased. Having witnessed how China challenged the US in the commons, particularly in space, the US must be certain not to lose this advantage in the face of competition in the future.

Finally, the United States has been willing to use its power not only to advance its interests but to promote humanitarian missions to advance the positive perception of the US. The US military is the Earth's "911 force"— it serves, *de facto*, as the world's first responder, an amalgamation of global police, paramedic, and fire department. Whenever there is a natural disaster, earthquake, flood, drought, volcanic eruption, typhoon, or tsunami, the United States assists the countries in need. In turn, this aids the US's power and security, as it favorably influences opinion of the US.[5]

Civilian and military US Defense senior decision-makers must possess an understanding of the principles of strategy and adhere to their dictates when formulating national security policy. First, international politics is defined by competition over power, which is necessary to advance its interest and to compel its will upon its enemies. Second, relative power and its distribution are more significant than absolute power. Third, maintaining US primacy is the core US interest because it protects the homeland and sustains the position of the US and its alliances. Due to the PRC's growth, and the delayed balancing against it, the relative distribution of power is shifting against the United States. If the US does not address this change, it will lose its position in international politics and face far greater security threats than it does today. These strategic fundamentals must be understood by decision-makers, particularly those who are too young to have experienced the Cold War.

Decision-makers must comprehend that competition is the ordering principle of international politics. This competition is based on an accurate understanding of the fundamentally conflicting interests of great powers. It is not the result of misunderstanding. Thus, international politics is cyclical, not teleological. Great powers are perpetually rising and declining, not advancing toward a final, millenarian end. The highest measure of success for the US national security community is to maintain the United States' current position for as long as possible.

US National Security Community Must Support the Education of New Generations of Strategists to Be the Architects of Victory

The US needs more and better strategists who understand power politics and the principles of strategy. Given the record of failure regarding the PRC's rise and the delayed and ineffective balancing against it, there is an immediate need to train and sustain a new cadre of strategists who are knowledgeable concerning the distribution of power and the principles of strategy to advance US national security interests in the current Cold War.

Good strategy is influenced by many factors, including history, strategic culture, regime type, organizations, bureaucracies, and many other aspects of the state and society with which it is concerned. However, most importantly, it is informed by people: the strategists—a coterie of strategic thinkers who, first, have been educated in strategic principles, including the distribution of power and net assessment; and second, who are tasked with ensuring victory in a competitive struggle. The United States does not have enough trained strategists to assist senior national security decision-makers to formulate a victorious strategy in the competition with China or with future peer competitive threats. The US national security community should study how it may better ensure that the US has the strategists it needs and to safeguard that each generation can train its successor. That generation-to-generation bond was broken after the Cold War with the Soviet Union, so younger generations do not readily have the required knowledge or mentors to introduce them to the issue and guide them through it. The service academies, and professional military education in general, have failed in this regard.

Such an analysis should be informed by seven components. First, power and its application in international politics must be understood, applied, and taught. A deeper training in power politics, diplomatic, military, and social history for a new generation of strategists is necessary so that they may identify the transient from the enduring, an inappropriate historical analogy or illustration from an accurate and fit one, and to guide the strategist's education in the theory of strategy.[6] The benefit of which von Clausewitz identified: "Theory then becomes a guide to anyone who wants to learn about war from books; it will light his way, ease his progress, train his judgment, and help him to avoid pitfalls . . . [it] is meant to educate the mind of the future commander, or more accurately, guide him in his self-education, not to accompany him to the battlefield."[7] The strategist should know when he is being fed a tactical answer to a strategic question, and be able to avoid intellectual fashions or *cul-de-sacs* that promise victory but have no hope of realizing it. Before the launch of his disastrous Spring 1917 offensive, French General Robert Nivelle promised to win the war on the Western Front in twenty-four hours, causing the great British historian Correlli Barnett to note thirty-six years later that "in despair men turn to quacks who promise them their dreams."[8]

Second, the breadth of strategic education is essential.[9] The strategist must recognize that cultural, ideational, social, and demographic issues are relevant as well. For example, abortion rates or alcoholism in the Soviet Union were key indicators that it was a weak society. Its citizenry was not invested in the future of society. That critical fact was almost wholly missed by Western strategists during the Cold War. Adverse social indicators of a stressed society should not be overlooked. Neither should language, including the importance of the English language for sustaining the US position in the world. Of course, to find these indicators requires looking in the mirror. The strategist is compelled to examine his or her own society, through a stark Cromwellian "warts and all" approach, for its weaknesses and vulnerabilities. Inevitably, this will require what is difficult to accomplish in any bureaucracy or in any society: interrogating ideological pieties and shibboleths. But the strategist must be able to accomplish it despite political pressure, groupthink, or accepted and unquestioned beliefs or cultural practices.

Third, strategists must assist practitioners as they seldom have the time or training to think strategically. Strategic theorists can do for US national security decision-makers what they need but cannot readily do.[10] The strategist should be able to provide decision-makers with strategic principles, advice, and options, as well as the collective wisdom or appropriate analogy that has been winnowed from the history of strategic thought. The strategist can help the practitioner by providing conceptual education that addresses the context of great power competition, how that context has changed over time, and why relevant concepts like power, relative power, and primacy is the foundation upon which US national security policy is constructed.

Fourth, the strategist is the guardian of strategic education for those in need of such education for their professional positions.[11] Part of this guardianship requires conveying knowledge of limitations and ignorance. Strategists can advise US national security decision-makers with respect to those opportunities or dangers that cannot be foreseen, and the ways in which the strategic effects of unwelcome surprises can be limited. This also means that the strategist must be aware of the variety of sources of friction and incorporate friction into defense planning.[12]

Fifth, strategy also requires the recruitment of good people with exceptional critical thinking abilities—as well as the willingness of senior strategists to mentor juniors.[13] The value of mentorship is easy to discount or not to identify at all. But it is a testament to his contributions in this endeavor that the late Andrew Marshall, the former Director of the Office of Net Assessment, clearly promoted it, as he reflected: "I think my major achievement is the training or impact I've had on the people who have come through the office."[14]

The knowledge one has acquired in the long course of a career cannot be easily passed on the next generation, but mentorship is more likely to make this possible due to the focused interaction between the mentor and more junior strategist. This situation is not unlike the loss of institutional memory, history, and a culture of problem solving that has affected the nuclear weapons labs. They have discovered the value of the having the "gray beards," older mentors, convey knowledge, culture, and history of the US nuclear arsenal and nuclear design and production facilities to younger scientists and engineers to permit a new generation understand how a host of technical and other problems were confronted and solved in the past. The point is not just to convey the history but also the culture that needs to surround the design and development of these complicated systems.

Most strategic education in the United States occurs in Joint Professional Military Education (JPME), that is, the War Colleges and National Defense University (NDU), by think tanks including Center for Strategic and International Studies (CSIS), Center for Strategic and Budgetary Analysis (CSBA), and Center for a New American Security (CNAS), or by small numbers of academics—largely at Columbia, Georgetown, George Washington, or Johns Hopkins University's School of Advanced International Studies. Despite the value of those institutions, this remains insufficient.

One essential element of JPME is providing military members a foundational level of understanding of the adversary nation. During the later stages of the Cold War in the 1980s all levels of DoD PME covered appropriate education on the Soviet Union and its military capabilities. At junior officer level (O-3) schools Soviet tactical and operation capabilities, weapons system capabilities, order of battle, and related topics were covered. The same education was also provided at the Command and Staff College (O-4) level. Thus, when students got to the War College (O-5) level, US military officers across all the services had a solid grounding in Soviet doctrine, tactics, politics, orders-of-battle, government, economics—and so had a solid foundation to understand the enemy.

The major problem regarding education about the CCP is that it is missing, as one former senior officer noted: "I don't think there was any education about communism or the CCP being a threat. If anything, it was thought that they were just a friend we hadn't brought around just yet. Too many officers learned about the PRC from Kissinger's books. There were also common cliches that 'China isn't really communist anymore,' 'They just want to make money.' Etc. That often seemed to be as far as education went or took most people. There were plenty of exceptions, but they were a real minority—and were considered cranks."[15]

This has not changed. Today, while there is some elementary training on Maoist military thought, the Department of Defense still lacks foundational education about the CCP, PRC, and the PLA. A major problem is that War Colleges must justify competence to standard civilian boards, requiring generalist education in security studies. While this is not necessarily a bad thing, by the time mid-ranking officers enter the War Colleges they enter with elementary knowledge of these concepts. This makes it very hard for instructors at the War Colleges to get to the complex level of analysis when students generally do not understand the basic governmental, political, military, ideology, history, or grand strategy of the PRC.

Even with the Secretary of Defense's 2019 direction to increase Great Power Competition (GPC) education within the DoD by 50 percent, it will still take another five to six years to integrate this training and education into the curriculum. US strategists and military planners are essentially ten to fifteen years behind on having a deep understanding of the PRC. As such, our thinking and actions associated with the balance of power strategy in the military domain will remain hindered as it has been for the past twenty years since the first indications of the PRC's trajectory were made manifest.

China and Russia devote more resources to the education and development of strategists than does the United States. While there is no simple correlation between the number of strategists and the strategic performance of the state, this study asserts that having well trained strategists in the right numbers throughout the government results in a more effective creation, critique, and use of strategy to advance the goals of the United States and to prepare for major and unexpected changes in world politics, including in the distribution of power, and to prevent or defeat future challenges.[16] But the United States does not have the numbers it should have, and so a priority for US national security decision-makers must be to expand strategic education.

Sixth, strategy is difficult because it is neither wholly political nor military, but the bridge between them, and thus the strategist must serve as the tenuous connecting tissue between political leaders and the military.[17] Moreover, strategists must study the weaknesses of their own society, military, and economy. Studying the weaknesses of one's own society is difficult to accomplish for two major reasons. First, it can be due to the strategist's familiarity and proximity to his or her own society. If not careful, the strategist may be more likely to assume or accept as implicit the political principles, economic ideas, cultural values, and social norms of his or her own society—what is commonly referred to as "mirror imaging." Second, alternatives or solutions may be invisible to analysts because they are accepted as givens when they are not. A strategist must be able to disconnect from his society and study it objectively and dispassionately as a natural scientist studies helium.

Finally, the US must have confidence that it can win in these anticipated peer competitive struggles. In the history of America's grand strategy, there have been many times when the United States seemed weak or in decline and unable to cope with the British threat, the Soviet threat, or the rise of Japan, China today, or some future threat. Equally, at these times, there were senior United States officials and experts in accord with this declinist sentiment. United States' senior decision-makers may not have such confidence due to their overestimation of the opponent's strength or an exaggeration of its own weakness.

The important role of strategist is to correct this so that US national security decision-makers have a clear understanding of US weaknesses and strengths. They must have confidence that they will be victorious in a long-term competition with a peer rival.[18] If the US is to maintain its position as the dominant state, US decision-makers must believe that engaging in the competition is the correct choice for the US and that they can defeat the challenge posed by the PRC.

The Necessity of Understanding Communist Ideology

"Know your enemy" is an eternal verity of strategy. A major part of knowing your enemy is understanding their ideology. The ideology of the PRC is Communism, which was well understood by the US and military during the Cold War with the Soviet Union. During that Cold War, the US national security community was educated in the tenets of Marxism-Leninism as it was essential to understand the motivations of the Communist Party of the Soviet Union, the Chinese Communist Party, as well as their key allies, such as Cuba, North Korea, and North Vietnam. It was also required to grasp their economic systems, domestic politics, the Communist International (Comintern), and after 1947 the Communist Information Bureau (Cominform) and relations with fraternal Communist parties. One of the authors toured the Soviet Union in 1987 and can attest that visitors from capitalist countries were lectured on Communist ideology. After the Soviet Union's fall, the study and knowledge of Communism waned in the US national security community.

Thus, there is an important juxtaposition of why Communism was well studied in the first Cold War but not in the years leading up to the second Cold War against the CCP. That absence of understanding contributed to the failure, first, to understand the hatred of the CCP for the US and their intent to destroy the US and, second, the failure to appreciate these points in the aftermath of 1991. Deng's honeyed words were what Gorbachev tried but failed to accomplish in the USSR, making his country stronger so that it could confront and defeat the US.

The ideology of the PRC explains its intention to defeat US national security interests globally, and why Beijing targets the US population and homeland. In the decades after the Cold War, US officials dismissed the PRC's Communist ideology as boilerplate, a legacy of the past that remained of diminishing utility while the PRC became a capitalist state, on its path toward becoming a democracy. As discussed above, the logic of the pro-CCP chool compelled trade, which in turn would advance human rights and democratic government in the PRC.

That was a Western conceit, and it helped the PRC's strategy of threat deflation. Far from abandoning its Communist ideology, the PRC has always sustained it—and at present is strengthening adherence to it under the guise of "Xi Jinping Thought." The PRC's Communist ideology has been and remains essential for comprehending its behavior. Accordingly, American civilian and military national security decision-makers must understand Marxist-Leninist thought, how Stalin contributed to that canon, and how Mao derived his ideology from Stalinism and its enforcers in the Comintern. Briefings regarding the history of Communism, the core ideas of its major thinkers, how the ideology drives conflict with Western states, and why the CCP believes that History is on its side, should be provided regularly, at all levels throughout the department. This is so that by the time an individual achieves a position of leadership they will fully understand the ideological origins of the current Cold War with the CCP.

For Leninism, the Communist Party would be the vanguard of the proletariat. The Party would seize the state and bring all else, such as social life, culture, and attitudes, under its control. The ultimate intent was to destroy bourgeois life, Western states, and Western civilization. The Bolshevik poet Alexander Blok's summation of the Bolshevik Revolution at its dawn in 1917 was "to *remake* everything." Remaking everything would require considerable force against the internal and external foes of the regime.

The PRC, of course, is defined by the Leninist path of Communism. The CCP and its ideology are entirely derivative from Leninism; it was formed and heavily influenced by the Comintern who led it, trained its key cadres, and resolved its major disputes. It is the stark truth that the Comintern and the Soviet Army brought the CCP to power in 1949.

The CCP is dependent upon the Soviets for more than bringing it to power. The Chinese Communist ideology of Maoism is also derived from Soviet sources. Mao took his arguments on the peasantry from Lenin's 1906 recognition of the necessary role that class could play in the revolution. Later, he took his ideas regarding the Cultural Revolution from left-wing Bolsheviks, including Alexander Bogdanov, and later Stalin in 1928 at the start of the first Five-Year Plan. It was Bogdanov and his allies on the Bolshevik left who made the argument, as Mao did forty years later, that the entire society—its attitudes, culture, history, customs, traditions, education, language, holidays, venerated historical figures, including statues, had to be remade through a cultural revolution to be in accord with what was politically correct—what the Party required.

Just as you cannot be a married bachelor, you cannot be a peaceful Leninist. By definition, Leninists of all forms are belligerent. They want to push their Hegelian/Marxist conception of History along to bring about the revolution in spite of Marx and Engels's identification of stages of class conflict. Leninists, including Xi, cannot accept other ideologies and are required to confront and defeat them. Fundamentally, they also must be aggressive as they are illegitimate forms of government. So, they must always have internal and external enemies to motivate their believers and sustain and justify their totalitarian grip on power.

For Communists, there has been a perpetual, restless aggression against the West since 1917. It was perfectly captured by Stalin's February 9, 1946, speech in which he delivered the first volley of the Cold War in a bold and sweeping address. He made three major points: first, Marxism-Leninism was fundamentally superior ideology and economic system to democratic capitalism; second, World War II was a test of all political systems and one that the Soviet system not only passed but in which it had proved its viability on the battlefield and in the sacrifices made by the Soviet people; and third, that war was inevitable as long as monopolistic capitalism existed.

As capitalism had caused both World Wars it would certainly cause the Third World War. Accordingly, the Soviet people had to prepare themselves for war, devoting themselves to achieve the goals of new Five-Year Plans. There would be no peace within the Soviet Union as the people would have to commit themselves to victory, and equally there could be no peace with the capitalist states. Stalin's speech was a shock to the allies, as World War II had ended with Japan's surrender only five months before.

When the sources of conflict due to the CCP's Communist ideology are understood, and that, perforce, the CCP is at war with the US, then senior national security decision-makers may understand that the CCP is inherently aggressive as Stalinism. Senior American defense officials must realize the value of political warfare for the CCP; that is, from the CCP's perspective, war is far more than kinetic. Anterior to kinetic war is political warfare, which is ubiquitous, unceasing even in kinetic war, and is the highest form of warfare. Political warfare subsumes kinetic war, which includes the Three Warfares— public opinion, psychological, and lawfare—touted by the CCP, as well as economic warfare, diplomatic warfare, and soft power.

Thus, the CCP's ideology drives the new Cold War, and it could not be otherwise—that is, for ideological reasons, the CCP must confront and defeat the US. Not taking the CCP's ideology seriously was and remains a common if profound mistake. The belief that increased wealth or engagement with the West would cure the CCP of Communism was, and remains, a major misunderstanding of Communist ideology. When US national security decision-makers see the world through a Leninist lens, they will understand why Communist ideology will always trump economic growth. They will comprehend why control over the Chinese people will always be a necessity, and, as in Hong Kong, valued over economic prosperity, or tolerance of "two systems." Finally, it permits US leadership to recognize that there can be no accommodation with the CCP. The US must fight to win the Cold War and must comprehend that the CCP will not end its struggle until it is defeated or victorious.

The Persistent Absence of Presidential Leadership

While the Soviet threat explains the entente with the PRC during the Cold War, the post-Cold War failure to defeat the CCP when the costs of doing so were far lower is the responsibility of the Clinton, Bush, and Obama administrations. The George H.W. Bush administration may be criticized for not moving to overthrow the CCP in the wake of Tiananmen. However, as we have argued, the cold logic of balancing against the Soviet threat and the uncertainty concerning whether Gorbachev would succeed in reforming the Soviet Union—which would make a more effective rival of the US—or whether he would be overthrown and replaced by a more belligerent Soviet leader, compelled a strong element of caution with respect to altering the relationship the PRC.

A stronger or more aggressive Soviet Union would require that Washington possesses an even stronger entente with the PRC. Only in the autumn of 1991 and winter of 1991–1992 is it clear that the Communist Party of the Soviet Union was moribund. The KGB and military would not overthrow Gorbachev but would permit the Soviet Union to break up and a Russian nationalist to replace the Communist Party. Although the transition away from the PRC was not as stark as required, the Bush administration did approve major arms sales, including F-16s, to Taiwan.

From Clinton until Trump, there was a consistent absence of presidential leadership regarding the PRC threat. President Trump recognized the PRC threat and attempted to address it. The Trump administration attempted to compel the inter-agency to recognize the danger to US national security and change decades of policy that worked, in a *de facto* sense, with the PRC to threat deflate.

As a consequence of the lack of presidential leadership, the attention of the national security actors was not centered on the growing threat when there was a chance to abort its rise through undermining or overthrowing the CCP or to adopt a range of competitive strategies before Trump to deter its economic expansion through the Belt and Road Initiative (BRI) or through territorial expansion in the South China Sea or Djibouti. As has been previously noted, other priorities were deemed more important at the time. While the PRC was seen as a theoretical future danger, virtually no one in the US government or associated agencies understood the immediacy of the threat. Even as late at 2019, senior officials within the Department of Defense were unaware of or denied the reality that the CCP was operating on their own timeline to achieve the Great Rejuvenation.

Presidents after George H.W. Bush until Trump chose to ignore the PRC threat, embrace engagement and the furthering of the PRC's economic growth and US business interests rather than strategic interests. This adherence to engagement greatly impacted US politics and the ability to perceive the threat and act against it. 9/11 and subsequent wars, and the failure of the intelligence community to compel the president's attention forcefully and consistently, resulted in rise of the PRC as a peer competitive threat with only modest balancing against the PRC at very little cost to the PRC.

The Failures of the US Intelligence Community and Military

Failures to adhere to power politics and the principles of strategy were sadly not the only mistakes made by the US. The US intelligence community and the military also made grievous errors that placed the US in the position of aiding its enemy while passively watching it grow in power, year after year. We consider the profound failures in the IC to identify and respond to the threat from the PRC and how benign assumptions about the objectives of the PRC have greatly damaged US national security.

Next, we turn to a major problem that affected the US military, the focus on the small war in Afghanistan and Iraq rather than the major war—so far, it is a cold war—that the US would fight with the PRC. Again, year after year, fighting wars in the western Balkans and the Global War on Terror had a profoundly negative impact on the ability to fight a major war against the PRC because of decisions undertaken by senior national security decision-makers. The concern was the war of today, not for the future war against the PRC. The unwillingness to accomplish both was a tremendous fault, the consequences of which we incur today. The victories in Iraq were hard-fought and costly in blood, treasure, and time, but they were transitory. The PRC threat is the existential threat, and the country is ill-prepared to fight a war with it due to the decisions made at this time.

The Failure of the Intelligence Community

Perhaps the best characterization of the purpose of having a national intelligence community was summarized eighty plus years ago by the now renowned US Navy Radio Intelligence Officer and principal architect of the US Navy's victory over the Imperial Japanese Navy at the Battle of Midway, Commander Joseph J. Rochefort. When speaking of the prime directive for any intelligence officer, Rochefort famously remarked "that an intelligence officer has one task, one job, one mission. This is to tell his commander, his superior, today, what the [enemies] are going to do tomorrow. This is his job. If he doesn't do this, then he's failed."[19]

As such, in the context of this study the failures of the IC were first to identify the PRC as an existential threat—this would have included identifying

Deng's political warfare strategy of threat deflation precisely as a political warfare strategy to obfuscate and conceal the PRC's vulnerability. Second, the IC
did not compel senior national security decision-makers to address the PRC
threat by illuminating the pernicious damage engagement policies were causing. At root, the IC aided Deng's political warfare strategy of threat deflation
because the IC had for decades consistently promoted threat deflation via
the policy of engagement. The IC never perceived the PRC through the lens
of the distribution of power; for many the notion that the PRC would ever
become a great power was always viewed through the lens of "decades away."
Then when the PRC's comprehensive national power had become undeniable,
even to the most ardent supporter of engagement, the IC chose to promote
the CCP supplied assertion that one must not "provoke" the PRC or else risk
thermonuclear war.

As a basis of national existence, the United States, like other nations,
depends upon its intelligence organizations to define the capabilities and
intentions of its enemies, and to aid the formulation of a response and measure its effectiveness. The US spends more than any other state to provide
US decision-makers with best sourced and reliable intelligence and has created an intelligence community with unrivaled abilities, skills, and talents.
When major intelligence failures occur, such as Pearl Harbor, the demise of
the Soviet Union and the end of the Cold War, before 9/11, and regarding
Iraqi Weapons of Mass Destruction (WMD) before the 2003 invasion, they
have always had mighty consequences for US national security interests and
compelled an explanation of how such colossal failures could have occured,
and what lessons should be learned to prevent their reoccurrence.

As significant as those failures were, they pale in comparison to the US's
greatest intelligence failure—the unchecked rise of the PRC. For a generation,
the IC failed national security decision-makers, and the American people,
regarding the growth of China's capabilities and intentions.

Appallingly, this failure occurred in plain sight. According to both the
World Bank, and the IMF World Economic Outlook database, China has
grown from about 1.6 percent of the world's gross domestic product in 1990
to about 19 percent today. Every year its economy grew without warning from
the IC of the consequences of this growth. The first of which is the CCP's

prioritization of funding for the PLA, which resulted in one of the largest expansions of military power by any nation on the planet since the end of WWII.

Indeed, the PRC's military has grown in every respect. The PRC's nuclear capabilities have grown from a modest force to one that in the first two years of the Biden administration, as noted by Admiral Charles Richard, former Commander of US Strategic Command, has had a "strategic breakout."[20] The rapid, yet still opaque growth of the PRC's nuclear arsenal may very well exceed the US's by 2030, if not sooner. Beijing already possesses more tactical nuclear weapons and theater forces than does the US. Its conventional capabilities challenge, if not dominate, the US military today in the Indo-Pacific, at sea, in the air, in the cyber domain, and in space. It utilizes this power to coerce Taiwan and Vietnam, as well as US allies, including Japan, Australia, and the Philippines. Beijing's diplomacy influences nations on every continent and from the Arctic to Antarctic. Its economic influence is ubiquitous, and is prevalent in the US as well, where Silicon Valley keeps close ties to Chinese entities and where Wall Street continues to permit Chinese firms raise capital on US markets, and US firms, such as Apple and General Motors, continue to invest in China. Where it is fair to say that today, the PRC's capabilities now match its Olympian ambitions.

As such, the Congress should investigate and demand an explanation of how senior national security officials and the US IC permitted the rise of a peer competitor without forcefully alerting decision-makers and the American people that this was occurring and framing options for the response. Given the resources provided, and esteem given to the IC, warning and options to address the PRC threat should have been provided, consistently, for decades. If certain elements of the IC were providing this, and it was ignored, then it is also important to understand why senior IC leaders in Washington chose not to act upon these indications and warnings.

Compelling the IC to explain this failure should be a priority for the Department of Defense, the Congressional China Committee, and the Senate and House Intelligence Committees. The administration and Congress should examine the failure of the IC and of previous presidencies to identify the PRC threat. The most important steps now are to understand how it could happen;

which assumptions were made about the strategic objectives and motivations of the CCP; what multiple failures occurred; why they could not be corrected internally by the IC; what assumptions and biases existed that colored the intelligence community's reporting on China; as well as understanding who understood the threat but was ignored or punished for accurate assessments of the threat.

Equally, the IC may be only part of this fiasco. If the IC was conveying accurate intelligence, including unhappy truths about how the pro-CCP school was aiding the PRC, to policymakers, then why this intelligence was ignored must also be understood. Explaining each of these bipartisan failures should be a priority of Congress and the Biden administration.

The greatest intelligence failure in US history occurred overtly, year after year, for two and a half decades because the IC failed to understand the malign intentions of the CCP—it simply did not take Communist ideology seriously—and made gross errors based upon benign assumptions of the CCP's strategic goals and objectives.

From as early as 1992 the PRC's senior leaders were revealing the CCP's strategic intentions to not only build aircraft carriers and build up their naval power, but that they were intent on using force to achieve their goals. For instance, in a September 1992 speech by PRC President and Vice CMC Chairman Yang Shangkun to the PLA General Staff, that was reported to have circulated among high PLA officers and was subsequently leaked to the *South China Morning Post*, stated that "China has decided to purchase an aircraft carrier within the next ten years as part of its attempts to become a major regional military power, and is prepared to use military force to settle territorial claims in the South China Sea."[21]

According to the *South China Morning Post*, a source who had read the entire speech stated that Yang went on to assert "hostile forces in the international arena may get burned by China if they do not behave well."[22] This small segment of Yang Shangkun's speech that was reported in the open press was just the tip of the iceberg from his entire speech to the PLA General Staff. Even after all these years, the contents of this speech have never been made available to the American public, even though there can be no risk to sources and methods by its release. This report is just one example of how the IC effectively buried information about the PRC's intentions to build up the PLA to assist directly in the CCP's grand strategy.

Another example of how the IC worked to hide the true intentions of the PRC came two years later in May 1994 when the *Washington Post* prominently featured an opinion editorial entitled "Inside China's Scary New Military-Industrial Complex" written by William C. Triplett, a former chief Republican counsel to the Senate Foreign Relations Committee (see Figure 1). In his opinion article, Triplett gave clear warning that "the West is about to be unpleasantly surprised by the emergence of a non-democratic military superpower in the world arena, armed with the most advanced nuclear and conventional arms."[23] The importance of this opinion article was that it documented the PLA industrial base build up was a real issue of concern as was recognized by the *Washington Post* as far back as May of 1994.

A LOOK AT... *Asia Past and Present*
Inside China's Scary New Military-Industrial Complex

By William C. Triplett II

Figure 1: Front page of *The Washington Post*'s May 8, 1994 "Outlook" section article, "Inside China's Scary New Military-Industrial Complex" by William C. Triplett II. Copyright © Thomas Kerr

Most concerning however was that IC officials recognized the importance of Triplett's warning article and immediately assigned a team, led by CIA China analyst John Culver, to "knock down" the assessment that the PRC was a strategic threat. Interestingly, in the ensuing weeks, Culver was still sufficiently annoyed from his tasking from the CIA that he announced to a room full of China experts at an annual unclassified PLA Conference in DC that he and his team had lost their weekend in "knocking it down."[24] Culver was manifestly wrong about the PRC in 1994 and has been his threat deflationist assessments about the PLA that dominated the CIA, the larger IC, and American senior leaders and policy-makers for the next twenty-five-plus years.

This is significant today because there are revisionists within the IC and academia who subtly assert that "nobody knew this" or "the Chinese only changed when Xi took over." These assertions are false, and if America is going to stay the course that President Trump set in motion, then historical accuracy must be maintained. Those who assert that "nobody knew" could have known, if they wanted to listen and examine the evidence, which they did not. Only willful blindness prevented it. It was all laid out thirty years ago in the "Outlook Section" of the *Washington Post* on a Sunday for the political class in Washington, DC, to read and to begin to adopt the required actions to prepare the US for the reality of threat the US confronts today. Those like Culver did not miss it; they purposefully closed their minds and denied it.

Secondly, the IC failed to follow the prime directive for intelligence professionals—knowing where the enemy is today and predicting where they will be tomorrow—out of fear of making a wrong predictive assessment. Americans have seen first-hand how the impact of the 2004 Iraq WMD Commission Report almost single-handedly transformed the IC when it came to predictive assessments about the PRC. Due to the WMD Commission's unrealistic requirement that IC assessments have irrefutable source validation, intelligence analysts—especially younger members of the community—began to hedge their assessments and pull back on predictive analysis for fear of coming to a wrong conclusion about what the PRC and PLA may do in the future, thus adversely affecting their careers.

The range and scope of this failure, to have deep understanding of the PRC, was not just confined to the activities inside China. One example of US intelligence community disfunction has been the refusal to acknowledge the PRC's role in assisting North Korea into becoming a nuclear missile state. As reported by Rick Fisher, senior fellow at the International Assessment and Strategy Center, "the PRC gave North Korea sophisticated 16-wheel trucks in late 2011 to transport its future intercontinental ballistic missiles. Those trucks have advanced through three generations of improvements and now carry North Korea's solid fuel ICBMs that are likely based on China's DF-41 multiple warhead capable ICBM."[25]

Another example of this PRC technology transfer were made manifest on September 8, 2023, when North Korea launched its first nuclear powered submarine, and the sail on the sub looks just like that on China's Type 039B submarine.[26] Not only has the US government failed to sanction the China Aerospace Science and Industry Corporation (CASIC) for the first transfer of ICBM transports, the US government has failed to articulate the severity of China's nuclear missile assistance to the North Korean dictatorship, and seize the political opportunity to lead a global campaign for all-around isolation of the CCP. That failure will have profound consequences. The US does not have enough tactical nuclear weapons to deter North Korea and China and cannot contain North Korean nuclear proliferation. This will make war more likely, first, in the Taiwan Strait and, second, when North Korea might be able to provide support for Chinese and Russian aggression by way of its own nuclear threats.[27]

Third, and most worrisome, is the IC's adoption of a defensive attitude whenever their analysis and assessments are challenged in the public domain. As it relates to the PRC, this defensive attitude from the IC was exposed to the public in 2000 when *Washington Times* reporter Bill Gertz wrote a column critical of the CIA's analysis of the PRC and how as a result "Congress had sought to set up a special panel of outside experts to challenge those within the CIA who were playing down the growing challenge posed by Communist China."[28] As reported, senior CIA analysts were "livid" at being exposed as being weak on China. This defensive reaction was exemplified when the then–CIA Deputy Director of Intelligence (DI), Winston P. Wiley, issued the following memorandum to CIA China analysts on October 27, 2000, which deserves to be quoted at length:

This morning's "Inside the Ring" in the *Washington Times* carries a story, "Target: CIA China Shop," that I feel compelled to address. In my thirty years as an intelligence officer I consider this the most blatant and undisguised effort to intimidate and politicize intelligence that I have witnessed. Simply put there is no substantive merit to the charges. The DI's track record on China bears the hallmarks of professionalism, meeting the highest standards of objectivity, impartiality, and trade-craft. Our work reflects deep expertise, is led by officers of the highest integrity, and has benefited from long-standing contact with outside experts. . . .

I believe these baseless charges threaten to undermine not only our work on China, but all of the serious and high quality analysis done by the men and women of this directorate. I met this morning with both the [Director of Central Intelligence] and [Deputy Director of Central Intelligence]. They share my outrage. They also share my view that the best defense against such efforts to undermine our integrity is to maintain the highest levels of tradecraft in all of our work. Each of you, from the newest recruit to our most senior office directors, needs to continue to be meticulous in your use of evidence, explicit in your reasoning, mindful of mindsets and preconceptions, and determined to call the shots like you see them—just like our China analysts have been. Meeting this high standard, which I see you do every day, is our best defense against politicization.[29]

These highly personal and defensive comments were not confined to just Deputy Director Wiley. Even more stunning were comments by then CIA analyst, and future acting Director of the CIA, Michael J. Morell, who reportedly wrote a memorandum asserting the CIA's China analysis was "a model of excellence and objectivity" and among "the best work" done by the entire CIA analytical bureaucracy.[30] By any metric, these two statements demonstrate a gross misreading and misunderstanding of the PRC. Rather than adhering to the prime directive that all US intelligence professionals have to seek truth from facts, to deeply understand the adversary and to warn about the potential threats to US national security, these statements reveal a worrisome, thin-skinned, and vindictive attitude senior IC officials had—and may still possess—toward anyone who questioned the IC's assessments on the PRC.

This vignette is not an exception to the rule, as one of the authors personally witnessed over the course of his career. This very same defensive attitude was prevalent among DC-based intelligence leadership, and their representatives in Hawaii, who spent more time trying to debunk and discredit challenges to IC assessment about the PRC than in objectively assessing whether such challenges might in fact be valid.

There are many examples of the suppression of dissenting opinions in the IC as it relates to the PRC, but the most memorable is the issue of whether the PRC would pursue and build an aircraft carrier program. As noted previously, as early as 1992 the IC should have been cognizant of the PRC's stated intent to have an aircraft carrier program, but even as late as 2006, senior members of the intelligence community had made it clear that the PRC would not pursue an aircraft carrier program for decades, if at all. The effect of such messaging was to degrade, dilute, and diminish IC collections, research, analysis, and ultimately reporting on this critical issue. Now less than twenty years later we know the results of this threat deflation; the PRC has put three aircraft carriers to sea in just over a decade. Unfortunately, this example was repeated time and again, always toward downgrading or denying the PRC's intentions or emerging capabilities.

Long gone where the days when intelligence analysts took large amounts of disparate pieces of source information and through experience, subject matter expertise, interpolation and extrapolation come up with objective, predictive and non-politicized assessments. As it relates to the PRC, the result of these factors within the US intelligence community has been a track record of underestimation and threat deflation at the strategic and operational levels of warfare.

Today, as US policy-makers assess the speed and sustainability of the PRC's expansion, it is therefore useful to look back on previous assessments the IC has made about the PRC's military power. Reasonably, we should expect to find errors and misjudgments when we look back—assessments of the future are hard, to paraphrase Yogi Berra—but the most notable feature of the IC's China assessments is that their misjudgments have been in the same direction, that is underestimating the PRC, perfectly fitting the definition of systematic error.

These errors have not been unnoticed, as former Commander of the US Pacific Command, Admiral Robert F. Willard, noted in 2009: "I would contend that in the past decade or so, China has exceeded most of our intelligence estimates of their military capability and capacity every year. They've grown at an unprecedented rate in those capabilities." Two years later, the Director of Naval Intelligence, Vice Admiral David J. Dorsett, similarly stated the PLA's emerging military capabilities have "entered operational capability quicker than we frequently project."[31]

As noted by retired US Marine Corps Colonel Grant Newsham, the intelligence community "had too many weak people who couldn't believe China wanted to destroy us or even harm us. And they had positions of power and held them for long periods of time—and ensured contrary analysis was suppressed. Or at best given a token hearing—and then ignored. Even military analysts were careful to downplay the threat so as not to 'roil' things in their organizations and chains of command—and get themselves in trouble."[32] The lamentable reality is that the US intelligence community, think tank analysts, and academics have an unfortunate track record of miscalculating the scope, scale, and timing of the PRC's modernization and its impact on US national security. As a result, the US, and the world, is now dealing with the consequences of PRC's rise, from the death of Americans from Chinese sourced fentanyl, off-shoring of American manufacturing jobs, coercion against Taiwan and the South China Sea, violence against India, exploitation of people and the environment due to its mercenary business practices, rampant intellectual property theft, and sustained deception about the origins of the Covid-19 pandemic.

The US and the world cannot abide more of these kinds of devastating acts from the PRC. It is time for an accounting as to how it is the IC failed. As was done during the Church and Pike Committees in the post-Watergate Era, the US intelligence community needs to be examined for these failures and systemic repairs enacted, not the least of which is an open rejection of the philosophy of threat deflation that has dominated the IC for the past thirty years.

The Failure of Military Leadership

Failures to recognize and prepare for the rise of the PRC are not limited to the IC—the Department of Defense, and specifically the uniformed military leadership, are also accountable for America's current state of unprepared-ness. A brief historic example will help put this into perspective. In 1949, as Americans recognized that the peace they had fought for in World War II was menaced by Stalin and the Communist Party of the Soviet Union, a small group of senior Navy officers openly challenged Department of Defense civil-ian leaders, the Army, and the Air Force over the strategy for defeating a Soviet invasion of Europe. The immediate issue was principally the prioritization and allocation of budget resources.

This challenge was called "The Revolt of the Admirals." The "revolt" was an effort to oppose the Air Force's preferred wartime strategy of relying on strate-gic bombing, specifically the B-36 bomber, to deliver nuclear weapons against Soviet targets and thus deter or halt a Soviet invasion of Western Europe. These Navy officers openly challenged the decision of the secretary of defense, whom they viewed as biased against the Navy, to cancel the US Navy's first "supercarrier," the USS *United States* (CVA-58). These principled Navy offi-cers believed this decision was not only harmful to the Navy's morale but, more importantly, was also detrimental to US national security.[33]

This history matters as evinced in a Congressional Research Service (CRS) updated edition (October 2023) of its report, "China Naval Modernization: Implications for US Navy Capabilities—Background and Issues for Congress." Importantly, this report included, again, the matrix labeled "Numbers of Certain Types of Chinese and US Ships Since 2005," herein known as "The Matrix" (see Table 1).

What "The Matrix" revealed is a glaringly obvious strategic trend line—where the US Navy is declining, the PLA Navy is clearly and unambiguously rising.[34] For example, the US Navy went from having a seventy-six-warship advantage in 2005 to having a deficiency of thirty-nine combatants for 2023 alone (this assessment is based on similar ship and submarine comparisons). As "The Matrix" exposes, over the course of eighteen years, there has been an overall swing of 115 naval combatants for the US Navy towards the PLA Navy, a strategic trend line that sees no serious interruption for at least the next decade.[35]

Today, the PLA Navy is the largest in the world, as has been concurrently documented, for the first time, in the 2021 annual Defense Department report to Congress on military and security developments involving the PRC.

Table 1. Numbers of Certain Types of Chinese and U.S. Ships Since 2005

Figures for Chinese ships taken from annual DOD reports on military and security developments involving China for the years 2005-2023

Principal Chinese combatant ships—*excludes auxiliary and support ships.* (The figure for total U.S. battle force ships shown toward the right *includes auxiliary and support ships, but excludes patrol craft.*)

Year of DOD report	Submarines			Surface combatants						Amphibious ships				China Coast Guard	Total U.S. battle force ships	U.S. vs. China
	SSB	SSN	SS	CV	CG	DD	FF	FFL	PC	LHA	LST/LPD	LSM	Total			
2005	1	6	51	0	0	21	43	0	51	0	20	23	216	n/a	292	+76
2006	1	5	50	0	0	25	45	0	45	0	25	25	221	n/a	281	+60
2007	1	5	53	0	0	25	47	0	41	0	25	25	222	n/a	281	+59
2008	1	5	54	0	0	29	45	0	45	0	26	28	233	n/a	279	+46
2009	2	6	54	0	0	27	48	0	70	0	27	28	262	n/a	282	+20
2010	2	6	54	0	0	25	49	0	85	0	27	28	276	n/a	285	+9
2011	2	5	49	0	0	26	53	0	86	0	27	28	276	n/a	288	+12
2012	2	5	48	0	0	26	53	0	86	0	28	23	271	n/a	284	+13
2013	3	5	49	1	0	23	52	0	85	0	29	26	273	n/a	287	+14
2014	3	5	51	1	0	24	49	8	85	0	29	28	283	n/a	285	+2
2015	4	5	53	1	0	21	52	15	86	0	29	28	294	n/a	289	-5
2016	4	5	57	1	0	23	52	23	86	0	30	22	303	n/a	271	-32
2017	4	5	54	1	0	21	56	23	88	0	34	21	317	185	275	-42
2018	4	5	57	1	0	28	51	28	86	0	33	23	306	240	279	-27
2019	4	6	50	1	0	33	54	42	86	0	37	22	335	248	286	-49
2020	4	6	46	2	1	32	49	49	86	0	37	21	333	255	290	-43
2021	6	9	56	2	1	32	48	51	86		57		348	223	296	-52
2022	6	9	56	2	6	36	45	50	84		57		351	224	294	-57
2023	6	6	47	2	8	42	47	50	60	3	57		328	142	289	-39
Change from 2005 to 2023																
	+5	0	-4	+2	+8	+21	+4	+50	+9		+17		+112	n/a	-3	-115

Table 1: **Sources:** Table prepared by CRS based on 2005-2023 editions of annual DOD report to Congress on military and security developments involving China (known for 2009 and prior editions as the report on China military power), and (for U.S. Navy ships) U.S. Navy data as presented in CRS Report RL32665, *Navy Force Structure and Shipbuilding Plans: Background and Issues for Congress,* by Ronald O'Rourke. Consistent with the DOD report, which shows data for China for the year prior to the report's publication date, the U.S. Navy data here shows data for the year prior to the prior to the DOD report's publication date. For example, the figure of 294 shown for the U.S. Navy for 2022 shows the number of U.S. Navy ships at the end of FY2021. As shown elsewhere in this CRS report, China reportedly commissioned its first two LHAs in 2021 and a third in 2022. The 2023 edition of the DOD report is the first to show a separate figure for LHAs.

This advantage is not just in numbers of warships and submarines, but it also includes raw tonnage, where the PLA Navy has commissioned more tonnage than the US Navy for most of the past decade. Add in platforms like the PLA Navy's 12,000-ton *Renhai*-class cruisers with its 112 vertical launch tubes for over-the-horizon weapons like the 300-kilometer ranged YJ-18 supersonic, anti-ship cruise missile (ASCM), and it is not a stretch to say that the PLA Navy now has achieved qualitative parity, if not superiority, in the ASCM arena with the US Navy.

This compels the question of how it could be that for nearly thirty years that senior uniformed members of the Department of Defense allowed this to happen. While there was a small cadre of Flag and General Officers who were cognizant of the rise of the PRC and the threat from the PLA, they were, as one retired officer noted, "swimming against the tide." The US Navy flag officer corps devolved from being an institution that had the moral integrity to "revolt" over principled disagreements about our national security strategy and budget allocation in 1949 to a US Navy today that is arguably outgunned by the PLA Navy without one admiral publicly speaking out in dissent or resigning.

While we have presented an examination of similar failures to warn and prepare for the rise of the PRC in the intelligence community, national security strategists, and even ultimately to successive presidential administrations, it is also worth noting the failure of our uniformed officials, especially our US Navy admirals, to "fight" for their service's unique equities and capabilities as it relates to the rise of the PLA Navy.

Despite the PRC's demonstrated disdain for human life, as witnessed at Tiananmen Square in 1989, there were other unambiguous indicators in the early 1990s of the CCP's intentions to build up the PLA and use it as CCP General Secretary Jiang Zemin called for against its "chief enemy," the United States.[36]

As with earlier warnings in 1994, in September 1994, the *New York Times* ran an article, again by Triplett, that effectively expressed concerns members of the US Senate were having regarding continued high-level PLA visits and engagement with the Pentagon and various elements of the US military. For instance, the report noted that "a group of high-ranking Chinese Army officers have toured American war colleges. As guests of the Pentagon, they are being briefed on the state of the art of US military technology and strategy." Triplett went on to warn that the "visit is the forerunner of a potentially dangerous program of military cooperation with China that the Clinton Administration has undertaken without informing Congress."[37]

Additionally, there were also reports of concern coming to Washington from "patriots in blue," junior officers at the deck-plate level from within the US Pacific Fleet who reported that Navy Admirals simply refused to believe the PRC was a threat. Throughout the decade of the 1990s, US Navy leaders in Washington and in Pearl Harbor seemingly went out of their way to provide their PLA Navy counterparts with what can only be described as an "open door" policy of access to US Navy ships and bases.[38]

The situation became so dire that by the end of the decade, there was so much "yelling and screaming on Capitol Hill" about the problem of the Pentagon's "open door" approach to military-to-military (mil-to-mil) engagement with the PLA that a series of specific "Thou Shalt Nots" were crafted from a bipartisan group from within the US Senate's Armed Services Committee (SASC).[39] The drafting of these "Thou Shalt Nots" was led by Senator Bob Smith (R-NH) along with strong support by Senator Daniel Inouye (D-HI) and Senator Ted Stevens (R-AK).[40]

Ultimately the Pentagon's refusal to curtail, or even reduce, its mil-to-mil engagement with the PLA led to the US Congress passing the 2000 National Defense Authorization Act (NDAA), which issued a series of restrictions to the Department of Defense that was designed to specifically limit the amount of mil-to-mil engagement between the US Department of Defense and the PLA. For instance, NDAA 2000 prohibited the Secretary of Defense from authorizing any military contact with the PLA that would "create a national security risk due to an inappropriate exposure" of the PLA to twelve operational areas of the US military: force projection operations; nuclear operations; advanced combined-arms and joint combat operations; advanced logistical operations; chemical and biological defense and other capabilities related to weapons of mass destruction; surveillance and reconnaissance operations; joint warfighting experiments and other activities related to transformations in warfare; military space operations; other advanced capabilities; arms sales or military-related technology transfers; release of classified or restricted information; and access to a DoD laboratory.[41]

As one Congressional veteran from this era remarked, "Can you imagine how bad things were for the US Congress to expressly forbid the Secretary of Defense and the Department from conducting these very clearly destructive engagement activities? Further, can you imagine the Congress ever having to issue such 'thou shalt nots' during the Cold War against the Soviet Union?"[42]

What is even more alarming is to understand that even with NDAA 2000 in place, the Department of Defense essentially found work-arounds to this Congressional oversight. For example, as personally experienced by one of the authors, during a February 2005 Hong Kong port call, a delegation of

PLA officers from the Hong Kong Garrison were invited aboard the USS *Kitty Hawk* for lunch and touring around the aircraft carrier (see Figure 2).[43] While the DoD and Navy undoubtedly believed they were following the letter of NDAA 2000, it is clear that they were not following the spirit of those restrictions.

Figure 2: PLA Navy Senior Captain Yang Wei Jun, aboard USS *Kitty Hawk* in port Hong Kong, February 5, 2005. *Photograph courtesy of the authors.*

Another instance was in 2007, when PLA Fleet Commander Admiral Wu Shengli was given tours of the US Navy's largest and most important East Coast base in Norfolk, Virginia, where the then–Chief of Naval Operations, Admiral Mike Mullen, ensured that Admiral Wu was allowed to visit a US Navy aircraft carrier and even a US nuclear submarine.[44] Feedback from first-hand observers indicated that for every 100 questions Admiral Wu and his delegation asked during these visits, they received 99 transparent answers from their American hosts. But such transparency was not reciprocated. Whenever a US officer would ask a question of their PLA Navy counterparts, they would be met with obfuscation or just no response.

In terms of why US Navy flag officers would adopt such a profoundly dangerous attitude toward unconstrained and unaccountable engagement with their PLA Navy counterparts, or their failure to understand evidence as contained in "The Matrix," and thus fight for building a Navy that could deter China's naval expansion and aggression, there are three main reasons.

First is the culture of the flag officer corps, which can be best described as "going along to get along." Long gone are the days when scrupulous flag officers like an Admiral Arleigh Burke, one of the original members of the "Revolt of the Admirals" as a captain, or an Admiral Hyman Rickover, the father of the nuclear navy, were promoted to positions of seniority and responsibility within the US Navy for their singular focus on the Soviet threat and the US Navy's ability to meet its missions in the face of potent Soviet naval and land-based power. This placed a great demand upon naval officers, NCOs, and men, and those who could not meet that demand were separated from the service.

What has replaced this era of principled service is a system of tutelage where officers are groomed for selection to flag rank based upon their obsequiousness and deference to the flag officers over them, despite their oath of allegiance to the Constitution and the principles for which it stands. This certainly does not reflect all officers. But the fact remains that for twenty years, not a single US Navy admiral spoke out in protest against the slide that was occurring to the US Navy, while the PLAN was concurrently growing faster than any navy since World War II.

That is in direct contrast to the Cold War, when admirals were acutely conscious of the growth of the Soviet Navy and conveyed that alarm in appropriate forums such as congressional testimony. Although now retired Admirals Michael Gilday and Richard, among others, have spoken about the China threat and the danger posed by that navy, their predecessors did not possess a focus on China's navy and its growing danger, year after year, to US national security interests. Naval shipbuilding and personnel have not been tested by the unending and prodigious demands of Cold War stresses, and so it is not known if today's Navy will meet them.

Second, as we have noted, is the impact of the pro-CCP school of thought, which argued that engagement with the PRC would normalize their behavior within the existing system of international norms that was created out of the aftermath of World War II and the Cold War. Not only were civilian analysts in the national security system susceptible to this philosophy of engagement, but stunningly so too has been a generation or more of US Navy admirals.

For example, just six days after the July 12, 2016, ruling by the PCA in the Hague that the PRC had "no possible entitlement" that would have justified China's environmental destruction, seizure of resources, and military construction within the exclusive economic zone of the Philippines, the then–US Navy Chief of Naval Operations (CNO) Admiral John Richardson was photographed in Beijing shaking the hand of PLA Navy Chief, Admiral Wu Shengli, the same Admiral that had masterminded the PRC's maritime revanchism against America's ally, the Republic of the Philippines in the South China Sea (see Figure 3).[45] Not unsurprisingly, the PRC propaganda machine loudly carried Admiral Wu's message that "China has no intention of stopping its island building campaign." At the same moment, PLA Navy ships were enjoying the hospitality of the international community at the Rim-of-the-Pacific (RIMPAC) exercises in Pearl Harbor, Hawaii.[46]

CNO Richardson's visit to China, in the aftermath of the PCA ruling, raises the question of the rationale for, and effectiveness of, the policy of mil-to-mil engagement with PRC. This reflexive response represents an ideological belief strongly held by senior US Navy, and other uniformed officers who sought to justify their ideological beliefs based on the thesis that says, "when they're talking, they aren't shootin'." Suggesting that if some engagement is good, then more must be better.[47]

Figure 3: Chief of Naval Operations (CNO) Adm. John Richardson meets with Adm. Wu Shengli, Commander of the People's Liberation Army Navy (PLAN), at the PLAN headquarters in Beijing, July 18, 2016. *US Navy (public domain)*

Accordingly, this pattern of thinking emerged. The former Vice Chairman of the Joint Chiefs of Staff Admiral Bill Owens demanded that "America must start treating China as a friend."[48] The former Director of National Intelligence and Pacific Command Commander, Admiral Dennis Blair, alleged that "Taiwan is the turd in the punchbowl of US-China relations."[49] Most recently, the current Indo-Pacific Commander Admiral John Aquilino speaking at length with *PBS News Hour* publicizing his numerous attempts to get his PLA counterparts to speak with him or in inviting the Chinese Navy to exercise RIMPAC in Hawaii.[50] US Navy admirals have demonstrated they put more faith in unconstrained engagement than they appear to take when it comes to fighting for the world's biggest and most powerful navy.

Third, and finally, there is the "frog in the pot" syndrome. In addition to the pernicious impact of going along to get along, the CCP has been very skillful in the timing and tempo of their military expansionism. Starting with Jiang Zemin's efforts to modernize the PLA, Hu Jintao's directives to the PLA to have the capability to take Taiwan by 2020, and on to Xi Jinping's overt operations like seizing Scarborough Shoal in 2012 to firing ballistic missiles around Taiwan in 2022, these actions were all done in a way so as to not compel the US Department of Defense into taking the actions necessary to mitigate the effects of this dramatic shift in the correlation of military forces in the Western Pacific. Hence, much like the proverbial frog in a pot of water, even as the temperature is raised one degree at a time until it is boiled to death, so too have US Navy admirals been numbed into inactivity against China as it seemed there was always a greater priority in the Middle East or Europe.

The collective impact of these three areas of failure has left America's national security today at great risk in the Indo-Pacific. The situation has become so undeniable, that even the then–Chief of Naval Operations Admiral Gilday's *Navigation Plan 2022* noted that America's security environment has witnessed an "erosion of credible military deterrence" particularly due to China's "investments in offensive warfighting systems—across all domains—are aimed at the heart of America's maritime power."[51] As the document rightly admits: "China designs its force for one purpose: to reshape the security environment to its advantage by denying the United States military access to the western Pacific and beyond."[52]

Hence, if there is conflict with the PRC, it will be on, over, and below the high seas, from Okinawa to Guam to Honolulu, all the way to the West Coast and into the US homeland. This will be a conflict the likes of which the US has not experienced since World War II.

Today US national security, in the face of this prodigious PRC threat, requires its own "Revolt of the Admirals" to explain how the US Navy arrived at this position of weakness against the enemy and to advance a plan to rebuild America's maritime power, just as American naval strategists did with the June 1940 "Naval Expansion Act," that dramatically funded and built the US Navy at the start of World War II.[53] Fundamentally, what is needed is a change of the culture of US flag and general officer corps so that the enemy may be confronted and defeated, not engaged.

Prioritization of the Minor War Today Over the Major One Tomorrow

A consistent and pernicious problem was the prioritization of the minor war fought by the US in the decades after the demise of the Soviet Union at the expense of the ever-growing threat from the PRC. The minor wars today against terrorists and insurgents were weighted over the peer competitive major war of tomorrow.

US Defense Secretary Robert Gates's comments on May 13, 2008, captured this well. Gates stated that meeting the warfighting needs of US forces today and taking care of them when they return home must be the priority of the US military rather than future threats including the PRC. The obvious concern here was that Secretary Gates saw the PRC as a future threat, not the immediate one it was.

In fact, the PRC was waging political warfare against the US and was doing so supremely successfully. From his remarks, Gates did not identify the enemy's prioritization of political warfare to defeat the US, thus making a kinetic war unnecessary as the PRC would be powerful enough to deter and compel the US as Beijing advanced its national security interests. The minor war today in Afghanistan or Iraq is always more important than the major war with the PRC later. Gates stated: "I have noticed too much of a tendency toward what might be called Next-War-itis—the propensity of much of the defense establishment to be in favor of what might be needed in a future conflict."[54] We employ this comment as an epigram for this chapter due to its importance as capturing this mindset.

For Gates, in a world of limited resources and budgets, the Department of Defense must concentrate on building a military that can fight smaller terrorist groups and militias waging irregular warfare. A consequence was delaying weapons that would be needed against the PRC or terminating them as Secretary Gates did with the Air Force's F-22 procurement and production line. For Gates, although he admitted that the US would be "hard-pressed" to fight any major conventional war at the time (2008), such a scenario was not likely and he believed, inaccurately, that the US possessed ample air- and naval power to defeat any adversary who aggressed, explicitly noting "in the Gulf, on the Korean Peninsula or in the Strait of Taiwan."[55] What might have been plausible in 2008 is certainly questionable today due to relentless PRC diplomatic, military, and territorial expansion.

The cost of the minor war focus came at the expense of the preparation for the major one against the PRC. The IC should have illuminated this painful trade-off and the risks it entailed for US national security. However, this falls to the president and the inter-agency. It would have required presidential leadership to order the Secretary to fight the minor wars in which the US was engaged, supporting units and individual soldiers when they returned, while preparing for the peer struggle against the PRC, and confronting the PRC to prevent its further expansion and rolling back its gains. It falls upon the national security community to be able to fight the wars in which it is engaged while preparing to deter and defeat the next foe.

Instead, the George H.W. Bush administration strategically kicked the can down the road beginning with Operation Desert Shield/Storm in 1991. Bush was not alone in this, as discussed above. Minor wars were fought against the terrorists and irregular forces that Gates identified at the cost of major war preparation. Not perceiving the nature of the PRC threat contributed to the inadequacies, weaknesses, and stresses the Department of Defense now faces in the struggle against the peer threat.

The Lack of the Examination of Assumptions

Related to the previous point, the Department of Defense also did not examine its assumptions regarding the PRC threat. There were three major assumptions that hindered the ability to define and respond to the PRC threat. Each had a significant effect and retarded the ability of the US to see the existential threat developing in clear sight.

First, there was an overarching assumption that history was at its end, and great power threats were an artifact of the past. The influence of the "End of History" mindset was considerable and gave rise to the conceit that the US was the acme of political and economic development and thus possessed the right structure to lead the world and cooperate with other states to assist them on the path to History's end.

Hence, as great power politics was of the past and did not frame the present, the "End of History" logic resulted in conclusion that the PRC would be positively transformed through the coterie of engagement policies, which included military-to-military cooperation. Such cooperation was supported by US Pacific Command leadership, including Admiral William "Fox" Fallon, who even invited PRC military observers to US exercises around Guam, and

Admiral Timothy Keating, who provided advice on carrier operations.[56] They were firm believers in mil-to-mil cooperation with the PLA.

Second, there was a bias that the US possesses the assumption of time to address future problems and existential threats to the US. For decades, there was always a more demanding task or issue to confront than the PRC threat. The PRC threat advanced relentlessly but relatively slowly in relation to the minor war of day, or the actions taken by Iran or North Korea, or the humanitarian or other crises which demanded immediate attention.

The third assumption was that the PRC would be positively transformed through the coterie of engagement policies as its ideology was not credible by the metric of the "End of History" and was not really believed by the CCP leadership, who it was believed were capitalists, and capitalism, despite a lagging effect, would result in greater freedom for the Chinese people. Too few analysts and senior officials took Communism seriously. A "Team B" group should have existed to "think like Communists" and provide different assumptions in order to provide contrasting analysis of the PRC's grand strategy and national security policies, how the CCP defined threats to their grand strategy, and the means they would employ to advance them.

Another set of problems linked to the third assumption is that analysts may become defensive around a certain narrative, such as the PRC's intentions are benign, or US actions compel the PRC's expansion and belligerence. Analysts are invested in an explanation or in a school of thought, such as the pro-CCP school, and so that school of thought must be defended. Thus, fundamental challenges to the pro-CCP school that necessarily will require major changes to US policies may be resisted. Focused leadership would be necessary to ensure that the intellectual framework analysts possess is altered in recognition of the enormity of the PRC threat to US national security.

The examination of assumptions is always difficult for an organization to accomplish, and more so when analysts are pressed for time in response to their day-to-day duties addressing major national security problems. The urgency and ubiquity of responding to the demands of day-to-day precludes time devoted to the focus on peer competitive, longer-term threats. With the necessity of having a constant attention to never-ending data, there is a reduction in thinking long-term. Presently, there is a constant focus on the daily briefing within the twenty-four-hour cycle of the Department of Defense. As such, there is little time for senior defense officials to think about long-term strategic issues, no matter how significant. In essence, analysts are on an endless treadmill.

Accordingly, there is value for a strategic team to be appropriately allocated to study national security threats within a longer-term period. For the Navy, for example, stronger connecting tissue between intelligence and operations so OPLANS would be informed by major threats without self-limiting thinking due to budget constraints or the preconceived assumptions already mentioned. The reason for having these analysts should not be to focus on immediate data or a brief but to consider emerging threats and significantly different scenarios to compel the questioning of assumptions and ensure that decisions are made in CONPLANS and OPLANS in the context of the principles of strategy. Thus, they are viewed through the lens of US power and maximizing US relative power over present and possible future adversaries so that US dominance is sustained.

Fundamentally, this is not a Department of Defense matter but is one for the National Security Council to formulate a national strategy that identifies the peer threat and marshals the government to respond. This must be beyond the policy guidance of published documents like the NSS or National Military Strategy or as it surfaces in QDRs. The Department of Defense may improve the identification of the peer threats through coordination of intelligence and operational plans.

Having been on the painful side of Napoleon's genius at their 1806 catastrophic defeat at Jena, the Prussians sought to institutionalize genius by creating a General Staff, as Trevor Dupuy analyzed in his exceptional book analyzing this issue.[57] While Napoleon charged a high tuition for the lessons he taught the Prussians, the Prussians, by institutionalizing genius in their General Staff, would be able to charge an even higher tuition for the lessons they taught Berlin's enemies in the nineteenth and twentieth centuries. In essence, the United States Department of Defense needs to do something similar; it must institutionalize Cato the Elder's insight. One that will always warn that the peer competitive threat must be identified, so that never again will the US suffer from threat deflation, and if the peer threat cannot be deterred, then it must be destroyed.

What the PRC Accomplished

The PRC leadership should be thanking their good fortune that they got away with it for so long. Indeed, it was to their great credit that they planned it so well. US and other Western elites would become heavily invested in the PRC growth, nurturing it for decades, while these elites gained lucre, returns to shareholders, and the trappings of wealth. The CCP leadership could not have imagined that it would be so successful to the point where even today there is a reluctance among American national security elites to balance as to do so would end their gravy train. In the back of their minds, the CCP leadership must have felt: "This is it; this is as far as the West will allow, they will start balancing the PRC now." Certainly, they possessed that concern under Trump, but with Biden, those fears must have eased. It remains to be seen whether the US will cause the CCP's fears to be realized.

Deng's Political Warfare Strategy Realized: The Insidious Problem of Elite Capture

Deng's political warfare strategy of "hide and bide" advanced from 1992 recognized that US elites could become invested in the PRC's rise. As US businesses and financiers became invested in the PRC's economic growth, they would become powerful allies in US domestic politics and in their international influence. Tying the PRC's growth to the pecuniary interests of much of the US elite was genius. Support for the political elite as well as the elite in media, the entertainment industry, foundations, and think tanks would be valuable for their direct and indirect influence on matters affecting the PRC, as Frank Gaffney has well documented.[58] US firms and Wall Street prospered through investment into the PRC, and the PRC used its wealth to support the US media and think tanks. In turn, through think tank personnel, meetings and seminars, and policy documents they helped to frame the ideas and assumptions upon which the US government relied to make decisions. Too many US politicians and officials, in addition to business, financiers, media, academics, think tanks, and foundations, were profiting from the PRC's rise and thus had an interest in threat deflation to maintain the status quo. As Newsham has explained to the authors: "I was also amazed that Deng's 'Hide capabilities and bide your time' was never ever recognized as a statement of

CCP intent towards us. He was basically saying 'we'll build ourselves up and kill you when we are ready to do so.'"[59]

In addition to US firms and Wall Street and the media, which proved to be a major barrier to defining the PRC threat, these same attitudes and financial interests have also seduced former US political leaders, cabinet members, and an assortment of officials from across the spectrum of our federal bureaucracy. These individuals believe they are the influencers, if not architects in many cases, of US policy toward the PRC during their time in each respective administration. What these "elites" have learned coming up the ranks of the civil or appointed service is that if they are not identified as critics of the CCP, then when they depart office, they can have a lucrative career as advisers or consultants for corporate executives or senior fellowships in think tanks that seek or conduct business in the PRC. The elites have been "captured" by the CCP, who ensures their efforts to support engagement will be supported by the Party either through direct financial renumeration or through personal notoriety as a "friend of China."

No better example of this "elite capture" was the July 2019 letter "Making China a US Enemy Is Counterproductive" to the *Washington Post* by MIT professor M. Taylor Fravel, former US ambassador to China J. Stapleton Roy, senior fellow at the Carnegie Endowment for International Peace Michael D. Swaine, former acting assistant secretary of state for East Asian and Pacific affairs Susan A. Thornton, and Harvard professor Ezra Vogel.[60] In addition to the authors, the letter was signed by more than eighty members of "the scholarly, foreign policy, military and business community, overwhelmingly from the United States, including many who have focused on Asia throughout our professional careers" and who felt compelled to expressed their "deep" concern about the growing deterioration in US relations with China, which they asserted does not serve American or global interests.

The evidence of their "elite capture" was contained in their list of "collective" views which ranged from "we do not believe that Beijing is an economic enemy or an existential national security threat that must be confronted in every sphere; nor is China a monolith, or the views of its leaders set in stone" to "the fear that Beijing will replace the United States as the global leader is exaggerated."[61] After decades of asserting the PLA was decades away from achieving even a modest modernization, the authors and signers of this letter boldly asserted, "Beijing's growing military capabilities have already eroded the United States' long-standing military preeminence in the Western Pacific. The best way to respond to this is not to engage in an open-ended arms race centered on offensive, deep-strike weapons and the virtually impossible goal of reasserting full-spectrum US dominance up to China's borders."[62] This attitude of defeatism and inevitable supremacy of the PRC are unavoidable indicators of just how effective Deng's grand strategy of "elite capture" had been executed over thirty years of American national security neglect.[63]

So it is that the career path of these appeasers was defined long ago by Henry Kissinger who had his own consulting firm, Kissinger Associates, a firm that from its genesis began escorting US business leaders to Beijing. Many former US officials have followed Kissinger's example. Clinton National Security Advisor Samuel Berger created Stonebridge International, which provided advice on the PRC. Madeleine Albright formed the Albright Stonebridge Group, and William Cohen created the Cohen Group. Hills & Co. is headed by former US Trade Representative Carla Hills. President George H.W. Bush's National Security Advisor Brent Scowcroft founded the Scowcroft Group, and Antony Blinken was a major figure at WestExec Advisors, but the dominant actor remains Kissinger Associates. Washington's leading law firms assist as well.

Consequently, for too long, US elites were content with the status quo— US manufacturing operations were moved to the PRC, where labor costs are low and corporate leaders do not have to worry about labor disputes with trade unions. That resulted in great returns for the US firms as well for the CCP and continued economic growth for the PRC.

The US was not alone of course, as European, Canadian, Japanese, and South Korean firms joined the march to manufacturing in the PRC. Australia provided natural resources. US allies in the Middle East supplied energy. By targeting Western elites, the PRC would ensure that the precursor to their growth, Western investment, continued, some of their wealth would return as investment in Western elites, and so balancing against the PRC was delayed, or even avoided in perpetuity.

This happy circumstance for the PRC would continue until the PRC would be powerful enough to recast the international order and advance its interests apart from concerns of balancing by the US. The PRC would be strong enough to deter or defeat the ability of the US to deny the PRC's national security interests. The Trump administration and Covid-19 upset this calculus, but it is not clear that the CCP's intent is yet on the path to defeat in so small part due to the tremendous influence of the pro-CCP school of thought in US and the West more broadly.

CHAPTER FOUR

WHAT THE US MUST DO

"We are going to do a terrible thing to you—we are going to deprive
you of an enemy."

> —Georgi Arbatov, May 1988 (senior "Amerikanist" in the
> Soviet Communist Party, who was Director, Institute of the
> USA and Canada of the Soviet Academy of Sciences and a
> prominent Soviet foreign policy advisor)

The problems identified in this book can be reduced to the simple fact that the
American national security establishment, from the president through the rest
of the responsible agencies within and surrounding the federal bureaucracy,
did not recognize the CCP as an existential threat and neglected to apply that
knowledge to America's foreign policy toward the PRC. As such, this chapter evaluates what the US must accomplish if it is to survive this existential
struggle.

The US must come to terms with Georgi Arbatov's declaration that the
Soviet Union would remove the existential threat from America's national
security elites. Without that threat, the US national security elites would
"lose the bubble," and focus on anything but peer competition.[1] Over the
past thirty years, the CCP successfully achieved this goal, which has severely
damaged US national security due to the death of strategy and the triumph of
complacency. What American national security elites must now do is admit
that they failed and must throw the rudder of the ship of state hard over—to
the principles of power politics vis-à-vis the PRC—if America and what it

embodies is to have any chance of survival against its CCP enemy. These elites must acknowledge that we have past the threshold of the "End of the End of History" and proceeded to the return to life as usual in international politics, that is defined by the "Normalcy of Great Power Competition"—and this will require a rebuilding and rearming of our national defense from reinstituting the principles of balance of power down to filling our empty arsenal of ammunition and strategic petroleum reserve.

In essence, today the United States faces the same reality as does a patient going to the doctor and being told that they have a cancerous tumor in their abdomen and that if left untreated they will die. The authors are acquainted with receiving such news and understand that no one who gets this diagnosis will ignore this life-threatening information, even for fear of the pain of treatment. Rather, a patient who understands and accepts the seriousness of the diagnosis will immediately begin to fight the cancer, be it with chemotherapy, radiation, or surgery. The cancer patient understands that if the treatments prescribed by the doctor are not followed, that the patient will die. So too is America standing today in the doctor's office and hearing that they have a cancer—elite capture by the CCP—and that this cancer must be treated and excised from the body politic. Those treatments will be varied, multiple, and painful.

Another apt comparison for the US national security community is to the famous Alcoholics Anonymous's "Twelve Steps for Alcoholics." The first step of which for the US national security community is to admit that they failed. The dominance of the Pax Americana that their strategic forefathers gave them, they lost. Hence, either of their own volition, led by a new president, or mandated by Congress—they must admit that they betrayed their mission; they did not recognize the existential threat of the PRC. Moreover, by promoting the engagement strategy of the pro-CCP school out of fear of provoking the PRC, they have strengthened the greatest national security threat the US has faced.

Second, Americans must understand the existing distribution of power within the US national security community is resistant to withdrawing from the pro-CCP school—their predilection will be to return the rudder of the ship of state to amidships and the course toward engagement with the PRC.

For example, the Committee on Foreign Investment in the United States (CFIUS), created in 1975 to lead a multi-agency review of the national security implications from foreign investments in American companies, has been largely irrelevant on the question of Chinese investment in America. Led by the Treasury Department, the committee's priorities have long been dominated by economic interests. While CFIUS became more active and focused on safeguarding America's national security during the Trump administration, under the Biden administration there has been a reversion back to the prior course of approving questionable sales of American companies to the PRC.

One instance that captures the point is the 2022 case of CFIUS review of DuPont's sale of its sustainable-materials business to a Chinese company. Despite objections by the Defense Department, and with "assurances" that the technology behind it is not transferred, the sale was approved by CFIUS.[2] This is just one example of many that could have prevented the transfer of valuable technologies, many of which end up in the hands of the PLA for use against our own military forces.

The solution is relatively simple: take the chairmanship of CFIUS away from Treasury and give it to the Defense Department. There are other areas where the federal bureaucracy could follow suit, but this is where the fight to change our system will be fought as the pro-CCP Engagers will resist such structural changes in order to maintain their lock on power. This "lock on power" must be systematically deconstructed and resistance from the pro-CCP school anticipated if the US is ever going to be able to survive what the CCP has planned for America.

Third, it should also be expected that executing this rudder change within the foreign policy community will take years of consistent effort to reverse—as can already be clearly seen from the sudden resumption of visits to the PRC by senior cabinet level officials from the Biden administration. Unfortunately, America does not have years to correct course. This Cold War with the PRC is not like the first Cold War because the strategists who built America's power during this fight with the Soviet Union experienced less resistance from the national security community compared to the present. Today, many American national security elites in and outside of the government are more interested in sustaining their involvement with the PRC—and because of this they will more actively fight against measures to confront and challenge Beijing's agenda of global expansionism.

Fourth, while significant challenges have been identified by this study, there is reason to be optimistic because of America and the great strengths that come from our Declaration, Constitution, and our almost two-and-a-half centuries of history. This history, defined by individual liberty, limited government, and moral responsibility, has proven superior and more durable than the incoherent, tyrannical, and failed political ideology of Communism, collectivism, and coercion that are the hallmarks of the PRC and the CCP's one-party state.

Fifth, America's victory over these internal and external forces is only possible if action is taken now. Given the shift in the balance of power toward Beijing and the existence of the CCP's "timeline" for the Great Rejuvenation, our nation's leaders must understand that action must be taken immediately to prevent the final destruction of the nation. The defense of the national interest from the war that is being waged by the CCP must be brought front and center and made a key part of our national political dialogue and selection of political leaders. Past policies promoted by the pro-CCP school that have been based on the false assumptions that the CCP's capabilities are "decades away" must be rejected, and there needs to be a sense of urgency and immediacy infused into our actions as a nation, across the whole of government.

Sixth, it needs to create a "Team B" dynamic to address the threat. Team B was created in the 1970s to challenge the IC's benign assumptions about the Soviet threat. Team B was composed of people from academe, industry, think tanks, and those with previous-governmental experience. It provided an alternative perspective, that the Soviet Union was aggressive and needed to be confronted. Thus, détente had to be rejected, as did policies of accommodation with the Soviet threat. In Team B were the seeds of President Reagan's solution to the Cold War: "We win, they lose."

A Team B for the PRC is needed that would bring together individuals from industry, scientists, negotiators, academics, and government service to create "quick fixes" to the immediate problems of the PRC threat. In the 1970s, Team B had a similar model of "quick fixes," to identify problems in the nuclear balance regarding targets, command and control, new technologies, and the survivability of strategic forces and propose potential solutions.[3] Multiple teams should be created to identify problems and suggest immediate solutions in the political, diplomatic, economic, technological, and military realms of the competition with the PRC. Too often, the US national security community has had a silo-based approach toward national security, the military operating in the military realm, the economic in its, and so on. What is needed is to get everyone in the same room, figuratively and literally, from across these domains, to identify the objective to defeating the CCP, and to devise and coordinate how to do so.

Seventh, in the Cold War, Soviet doctrine was well studied by the US national security community to discern where the Soviets were investing, what they were developing, and the force structure they were creating and the missions that force structure could support. Today, the US needs to have the same familiarity with the PLA's doctrine to understand their priorities for investment, research, and force structure development, and the missions and options that force structure would support. Information about this should be brought into the public sphere to inform the debate regarding the PRC's bellicosity and capabilities for aggression.

Eighth, given the CCP's unambiguous development of a nuclear first-strike capability, the US needs to support nuclear proliferation in the case of Japan, South Korea, and Taiwan to complicate the PRC's strategic calculus. Nuclear proliferation introduces considerable risks, notably the incentive of the PRC to arrest it, including by military action, before a state becomes nuclear. But the benefits for the US as well as for these states is that each would have a strong deterrent. Nuclear deterrence is the product of capabilities like a secure second-strike and survivable command and control, but also political considerations like the willpower and credibility of the state—and the balance of resolve: who values the territory more.

There are four major advantages for stability in East Asia. First, were Tokyo, Seoul, and Taipei nuclear, then the PRC could not doubt that each would respond if attacked. The balance of resolve would clearly favor these states. Second, in contrast with an extended deterrent from the US, there may be doubts in Beijing that the US would honor its extended deterrent commitments, so the new nuclear states strengthen US defense posture in the region.

Third, as new nuclear states, the US would benefit as the danger of PRC retaliation against the US homeland would be reduced. Fourth, the PRC's ability to coerce these states would also be reduced and their ability to maintain their sovereignty over territory disputed by Beijing would be greatly augmented as the balance of resolve would be heavily weighted to them.

Ninth, the US needs to take bold action to target the CCP directly.[4] This requires a multifaceted approach that will include the rollback the PRC's gains in the South China Sea and the defeat of the PRC in its attempts at future territorial seizure like the PRC is currently conducting against the Philippines at Second Thomas Shoal. The US and its allies should even be prepared to evict the PLA from facilities they have created in other countries like Djibouti, or are in the process of creating in Ream, Cambodia. Those are important and necessary measures to place Beijing on the strategic backfoot. But the center of gravity that the US must attack is the CCP itself to ensure that the CCP, the Chinese people, and all global audiences know that it is illegitimate and that the US, working with the Chinese people and allies, is working to expel it from power. This requires employing all the arrows in the US quiver, including a focus on political warfare that the US did well during much of the Cold War but has allowed to fall into disrepair in the post-Cold War years.

These various tasks must be synchronized—the "it will take years" to fix, while true to a degree, cannot overshadow or retard the impetus to act today, across all levers of national power. In essence, Americans must recognize that we are truly, for the first time since the Cold War, in an existential fight for our national survival.

CHAPTER FIVE

WHICH SIDE ARE YOU ON—
THE CCP'S OR AMERICA'S?

Strategic mistakes do not come much bigger. In a historically unprecedented act—truly without parallel as great powers simply do not make such fundamental errors—the US contributed mightily to the creation of its most formidable peer competitor. Thus, the greatest strategic mistake made by the United States in its long history was to ignore changes in the relative distribution of power with the PRC. The US has failed to advance its principal interest in international politics: preventing the rise of a peer competitor. It is difficult to comprehend the enormity of the blunder, but Americans must, while facing the cold truth that it happened.

In the wake of the Cold War, the United States believed itself to be in the Hegelian "End of History," in which great power competition would be absent as the US remained the world's sole superpower. The US was free to further the PRC's economic growth through investment in manufacturing, the transfer of intellectual property and technology, while strategic considerations were not at the center of decision-makers' considerations. Year after year, the relative distribution of power with the PRC gradually changed in Beijing's favor. Everyone saw this occurring, yet almost no one fought it. Far too many among the elite celebrated and profited from it.

Countless Sinologists, foundations, think thank denizens, Silicon Valley and Wall Street gurus, and gormless US analysts and policy-makers contributed to this inexcusable failure to recognize the threat. As a result of their failure, the greatest national security challenge is now before the US. Through their collective failure, they have saddled the US national security community, the American people, and their global allies with a new Cold War. A war whose costs will be mighty and whose victorious outcome is in doubt.

It is both appalling and shameful that US decision-makers labored to create this challenger. Warnings of this adverse change in the distribution of power were not heeded by US decision-makers. To the contrary, the US government, the business community and Wall Street, and the Sinologists in the academy promoted and pursued policies which emphasized coopera-tion, "bringing China in" to the international order and fostering its growth, so that it would become a "responsible stakeholder." For many in the pro-CCP camp, there was an altruistic expectation that China would cooperate with the West to preserve the present liberal order of global politics. For others, their recommendations were based on individual greed and avarice. Regardless of the motivation, there have always been illusions about China— particularly this unproven notion that China is becoming like the US. For example, "With God's help, we will lift Shanghai up and up until it is just like Kansas City," Senator Kenneth Wherry of Nebraska declared during Chiang Kai-shek's rule of a unified China.[1] Unfortunately, the illusion that the PRC would become a responsible stakeholder has been as close to fatal as any other such international relations theory ever adopted, and indeed it very well might be.

This approach was naïve and a profound and lasting mistake. As Deng intended with his political warfare strategy, it permitted the PRC to hide behind a false promise to abide by Western rules and norms to forestall bal-ancing against it while it rapidly developed economically and militarily—and creating a new international order to replace the Western, liberal one. Despite the claims to the contrary, the PRC is not a *status quo* great power. It is truly a revolutionary great power that seeks fundamental and permanent changes to the contemporary order in international politics.

For decades, US national security decision-makers viewed international politics and the position of the US in it through the lens of an inexorable movement toward democracy and free market economics.[2] This idealistic view was disastrous for US national security policy. Indeed, it remains so, as it still contributes to a delayed response to China's expansion, and if not corrected, might prove fatal to the US. The "End of History" paradigm is fundamentally pernicious. It is as intellectually disarming as it is wrong. It contributed to a dangerously sanguine and self-satisfied view of the US position in the world, while ignoring strategic principles. These beliefs contributed indirectly to venality and the corruption of the US political system. As Deng said, "to get rich is glorious," and the US elite did not have to be told twice.

The PRC was masterful in its identification of US domestic weaknesses—the lure of cheap manufacturing in the PRC would be too great a temptation for US firms, particularly as Japanese and South Korean firms were already present, and there already was established cooperation in the defense industry. Once that threshold was crossed, it was practically impossible to stop even if a US president wanted to end it. The PRC has become the most formidable opponent the United States has faced, and how such massive threat deflation of the China occurred for the generation after the Cold War's end must be thoroughly understood. Such strategic malpractice must never happen again if the US is able to defeat the CCP.

The leadership of the CCP prepared the political warfare battlespace with genius. As we have shown, under Deng, China expertly, even perfectly, concealed their intent and capabilities while manipulating the stronger state. To his credit, Deng's strategic principles, captured in the 24- and 28-Character strategic aphorisms, were realistic and fully acknowledged power politics: The PRC was weak and confronted a precarious situation. With the conclusion of the Cold War, and with the absence of the Soviet threat, the PRC was vulnerable to US pressure for significant reform of the CCP and pressure to democratize. Beijing needed favorable conditions for its development.

Accordingly, a confrontational approach by the CCP was not an option. As the PRC was not yet a great power, Beijing had to avoid being a target while Deng laid the foundation for a peer competitive challenge to the United States. His strategic narrative contributed to the West's inability to identify Beijing as a threat. While avoiding military entanglements in the region and, especially, with the United States, Beijing eagerly pursued—free from any serious balancing against it—the political and economic opportunities available to a rising power within the international system created by the United States.

The United States cannot fault its foe from employing every means at its disposal to deceive US decision-makers and the American people, as well as to use US power to aid its rise. Our book has demonstrated that the fault lies with US decision-makers over the last thirty years. Broadly, the United States intelligence community failed, and thus the US faces its current precarious situation. This was a bipartisan failure, for which Democrats and Republicans alike are responsible as both abetted the PRCs rise and were unable or unwilling to reveal the PRC's deception or its true ambitions.

If US national security interests and the liberal order are to be saved, it will be by confronting and defeating the PRC's challenge to it. Until recently, the confrontation has been largely one-sided. The PRC acted vigorously to undermine the position of the West, while the West's response was largely absent, inchoate, or even pernicious to its strategic interests. The most charitable interpretation of why the United States did not balance against the PRC was that it had a gross misapprehension of what US national security interests were. Put succinctly: US decision-makers had a profound misconception of the fundamental principles of power politics, the need to sustain US primacy, and defeat the threat from the ideology of Communism.

Fundamentally, the United States did not respond to the challenge for three reasons. First, the economic interest of US and other Western business communities. The PRC's rise was aided by its ability to influence Western firms in the PRC, trading access to the PRC's enormous market in return for the firms' knowledge, technology, and processes. At the same time, the PRC employed the firms' influence with their domestic governments to ensure support for the PRC. Second, what the Chinese could not willingly receive from economic cooperation they would steal through bribery, extortion, or the development and employment of their advanced and persistent cyber capabilities. Third, the rise of the PRC was met by a historically unique case of threat deflation in the United States. This was due to the PRC's deception through its projection of an image of itself as a benign developing power that fully embraced the liberal international order, only seeking to be a responsible stakeholder. The US consistently and gravely underestimated the dangers and implications of the PRC's rise, including how it will change international politics, and its ability to hold at risk long-standing US principles of individual liberty, consent of the governed, separation of powers, checks and balances, and equality under the law.

These failures compel an accounting in two respects. First, it is important as a matter of the historical record to document who said what about the PRC, or the lack of a PRC threat, and when did they say it, and to ensure that this grossly mistaken analysis and advice is never again heeded. Second, the failure of the US national security community reflects a larger moral corruption of America and the success of the CCP's Communist agenda. In the 1996 campaign, Senator Bob Dole asked plaintively "Where's the outrage?" when the Clinton campaign corruption began to surface. He was frustrated that no one seemed to care that the PRC bought influence with Clinton. Moral opprobrium was not sufficient to prevent Clinton's reelection.

Since that time, the outrage that would have been volcanic in the Cold War has faded further. Today, New York financial analysts might worry about whether a firm is involved with contributing to climate change, but they are not concerned whether it is involved with the CCP. That must change. Chinese firms are still traded and allowed to raise capital on US and other Western markets. They should not be—because that money is being used to build the PRC's capabilities to destroy the US—like the PLA, for instance.

Gandhi had the "Quit India" campaign to pressure the British into leaving India, and the 1980s witnessed the divestment movement for firms that traded with *apartheid* South Africa, so the US and its allies could have a "Divest CCP" movement. Divestiture is essential as many PRC entities profit directly or indirectly from ties with the PRC military, or do not recognize human rights of the Chinese people and profit from the coerced labor of the Chinese Muslim concentration camps. Such entities ought to be ejected from Wall Street.

Absent an understanding of the ideological threat and moral offensiveness of the CCP, it will be difficult to implement the whole of society response that is so desperately needed. Too many of the elite have either lost their moral compass, their comprehension of the duties and obligations of the citizen in the American republic, and their understanding of American national security interests. Or perhaps they never possessed or supported these principles. That is a broad failure of American institutions, including most importantly of the educational system to teach the history of the US's stand against tyranny. Too many see the CCP as a partner. They are blindly nurturing a crocodile that will have no hesitation to eat them too.

A lesson from history is: do not help your enemy. The recognition of this alone would be sufficient to prevent the visit of the Secretary of Commerce Gina Raimondo, who seeks to save the $700 billion US-PRC trade relationship at a time when the CCP is supremely vulnerable and amid several crises, including a major economic downturn, that have the potential to test the Party's grip on power.[3] The world has not had such an opportunity since the 1989 Tiananmen Square massacre.

Yet, instead of developing a strategy to accelerate the demise of the CCP, the Biden administration is assisting the PRC's economy from collapsing. Secretary Raimondo's visit joins a panoply of high-level Biden administration visitors to the PRC over the summer of 2023, at the very time the CCP's grip on power could be pried loose—and thus liberate the people of China and the rest of the world. The stated purpose of this cavalcade of visits from Antony Blinken, Janet Yellen, and John Kerry was to re-establish "dialogue," but are instead unseemly and not appropriate for representatives of the United States.

At root, they are an attempt to return to the Old Regime that governed the US's policy toward the PRC for over a generation. This was the Kissinger School of Engagement with the PRC, what we have labeled throughout this book as the "pro-CCP school," and for the past thirty years it saw no downside to the flow of cooperation, investment, and knowledge transfer to the China as year after year the PRC became stronger and the US, in relative terms, became weaker. For them, the CCP is a partner.

But that is the rub. The pro-CCP school does not perceive the CCP to be their enemy. Instead, they view the CCP as a loyal associate in wealth creation, including the creation of their personal wealth. Accordingly, for the pro-CCP school, a dollar invested in the PRC is well spent as it would provide a higher return. Unfortunately, the costs, including opportunity cost, of not investing in the US was not considered.

Manifestly not considered was the odious nature of the CCP as a form of government. The pro-CCP school did not see engagement with the CCP as a barrier to US national security, but a plus. For the "CCPers," the CCP's tyranny ensured there was political stability for profits to be made and their oppression and gross human rights violations directed against the Chinese people have been and continue to be ignored. After decades of benefiting handsomely, American elites like the late, Henry Kissinger, Raimondo, Hank Paulson, Jack Lew, Timothy Geithner, Steve Orlins, Stephen Roach, and many others who have profited are in a place to assist the CCP out of its economic crisis, caused by its own failed system, by lifting Trump's trade restrictions and keeping capital flowing to the PRC's entities. Helping their CCP partners is nothing more than a return to business as usual.

This return to "business as usual" was made explicitly clear by Joe Biden during a press conference in Vietnam on September 10, 2023, when he said, "I'm not—we're not looking to hurt China, sincerely. We're all better off if China does well—if China does well by the international rules. It grows the economy."[4] The fact the Biden administration seeks to return to the failed—and the almost fatal for the US—policy of engagement as we have stressed in this book is pro-CCP and reveals that their interest is with the CCP rather than its opponents. That places the Biden administration in opposition to those who seek to free the world from the greatest source of belligerence in international politics and of political tyranny. Plainly, that is a not a place an American administration should ever be. The fact the administration is in such a spot is curious, as is the fact that they seek to aid rather than overthrow the CCP.

If you see the CCP as the enemy, now is the time to maximize pressure upon it in every realm, as it is under great stress. Much needs to be done, but most importantly the US response must be organized, focused, inspiring, and educational. In essence, what is needed is a new Truman Doctrine to aid any country, entity, or group fighting the CCP. As a result of Soviet coercion directed against Greece and Turkey, the 1947 Truman Doctrine stated that the US would help any country resist Soviet expansion. The value of a doctrine is that it can clarify the nature of the enemy and the need for all Americans to counter it, task the national security bureaucracy, and work in conjunction with formal allies and informal supporters around the world.

A modern Truman Doctrine would provide an ordering principle for US governmental audiences and the American people, as well as with international audiences, and help the US organize its response to the CCP with a focus and coherence that has been absent with the Biden administration.

A contemporary Truman Doctrine would ensure Taiwan has the capability necessary to provide a conventional deterrent to a PRC invasion. A new Truman Doctrine would energize the necessity of standing with the Filipinos, already a treaty ally, as they resist the PRC's recently resurgent aggression at Second Thomas Shoal and provide a path forward to work with the Filipinos to reverse the PRC's earlier illegal seizure of Filipino territory at Mischief Reef and Scarborough Shoal.

In the economic realm, such a clear statement would assist the necessary steps of cutting the PRC out of the Wall Street and New York financial markets so the CCP and all PRC entities, including in Hong Kong, receive not a cent, and moving toward ending trade with the PRC.

In the sphere of domestic politics, a modern-day Truman Doctrine would provide Americans with an understanding that the PRC is the enemy as well as draw a stark contrast with those who seek to support the enemy and those who want to defeat it.

The issue is clear: which side are you on, America's or the CCP's? This is as compelling for every American as it was during the Cold War: freedom and liberty versus control and slavery.

The American people and their foreign policy cannot continue on this course. The country is riven by an elite that still seeks to support the CCP and will permit the strategic opportunity presented by their own abuse, misrule, and oppression, to pass. In contrast, those who perceive the threat to the United States seek to capitalize upon the opportunity provided. Biden's inaction will save the CCP in a moment of profound crisis. If this opportunity were to pass without any action, then US relative power vis-à-vis the PRC will continue to decline.

It is not too late for the United States to act. If US primacy is to be preserved and protected, it is incumbent upon the United States to defeat the PRC's ambitions. This will require embracing the strategic principles of power politics illuminated in this study. Just as importantly, strategic analysis compels the recognition that the defeat of the PRC will not be final victory. There are no final victories in international politics as relative power is always shifting, at times with great rapidity as the world witnessed with the PRC's rise. Thus, the sustaining a favorable distribution of power requires acute sensitivity to relative power by the IC and senior national security decision-makers.

If the US is victorious in its fight with the PRC, it may enter new period of competition with a future great power. Accordingly, the US must heed the lessons of its grievous mistakes made with China's rise to dissuade or prevent a new peer competitive challenge as well as to advance and sustain the other strategic interests in the Indo-Pacific and globally. All interactions with potential rivals must be governed by the principles of strategy. This requires an acute sensitivity for relative power. US decision-makers in every realm—diplomatic, economic, military, technological—must query not "will all sides gain" but "which party will gain more" from trade or cooperation. The US must focus on its dominance and political-military measures necessary to preserve it. Never again can US decision-makers let trade and economic interests undermine US permanent strategic interests.

We have stressed that there must be an accounting of how the US could permit itself to lose the strategic dominance in enjoyed in the 1990s with the position it faces today. To avoid such an error again, three subjects must be addressed.

First, the US must focus on the relative distribution of power as its primary concern in its evaluation of threats but also of military aid, cooperative agreements, and approval of technology transfers. The concern for the relative distribution of power must be an iron law for the IC, the US State, Defense, Treasury, Justice, Energy, and Commerce Departments, indeed, all of the "Ds & As" in the US government, and that broader US national security community. That iron law must also govern the actions of centers of intellectual knowledge, technological innovation, and US businesses and financial markets.

Second, the US national security community should add its weighty voice to advance the sinews of national power, most importantly to education in the principles and history of power politics, the history and ideology of Communism, and the value of US primacy. These topics need to be taught in professional military education and reflected in the professional journals of the services. A key element of the educations of officers is to view international politics through the lens of power politics with an acute appreciation of relative power.

Third, upon reflection of the US's gross malpractice in statesmanship, there are three hard lessons for the US. First, that it must never again threat deflate; second, the country's leaders and its elites must recognize that great power politics never stops, there is no terminus, relative power is always changing among the great powers; and third, the US national security establishment must adapt quickly and skillfully to defeat the next rising threat. The US's relationship with any great power must be defined not only through the immediate relationship based on the threat from the PRC but also though winning the peace once the PRC is defeated. The US national security establishment has not demonstrated the intellectual nimbleness to adapt to the cycle of power politics—peer threats rise, are defeated through the application of US and allied power, then members of that successful coalition are likely to become the next peer threat for the United States, as the PRC did.

There is an inclination in US strategic thought to see international politics through the teleological lens—the threat is defeated, proving US superiority, which permits a relaxation and even an end to great power security concerns. Until that is corrected, the US remains vulnerable to manipulation through threat deflation and thus provides for itself the Herculean challenge of once again having to defeat a peer competitor, with the prodigious risks this entails, rather than the relatively easier task of preventing the peer's rise.

These actions will take considerable time. To reform JPME alone will take time to change the administration, professors, curriculum, and readings. Nonetheless, this must commence now. In essence, the US government and the America elites must go through a detox program to break their dependency on the CCP. That must be a whole of government and whole of the American elite response to this problem.

We expect that the response will be uneven, with some in the national security community responding with alacrity, but inertia and the desire to profit are powerful forces. For these reasons alone, the remainder of the US government and of US society will be harder to change.

If there is a major crisis or war, then the true nature of the CCP will be revealed, and perhaps only then will its threat be assessed accurately by the whole of the elites in US society. In the event of war, the demands for accountability will be incandescent and filled with rage for those today touting engagement. That is a terrible price to incur, and we hope that it may be avoided.

Indeed, one of the objectives of this book is to call attention to the problems so that they may be addressed before a major crisis like the Cuban Missile Crisis, or a limited or major war. Absent profound reform in the wake of a crisis or war, to cause the necessary change before those horrific events will require new leadership such as the return of President Trump to identify the enemy, sustain the focus on it, and require the government and the elite to respond accordingly. That is a difficult but necessary task. It is also one that must be executed immediately, as the time lost since the Trump years carries its own costs.

The solution is no less than securing a new elite for the country, and certainly a new national security elite that understands power politics and why the distribution of power is the engine of international politics, and that comprehends the ideology of Communism and so grasps the true nature of the threat faced by the United States.

However, much has changed since 1991—no less so than the American elite. The business and financial elite were instrumental in driving investment in the PRC and assisting its rise. They are a core constituency of pro-CCP school and have consistently sought to profit in the PRC and have used their wealth to influence American politics.

As the Cold War receded and Americans knowledge of Communism faded, to the mix was added an elite that was positively disposed to the CCP for ideological reasons. This elite admired the CCP either because they were "efficient," as an Elon Musk or Bill Gates might identify, or because they were supportive of Communism and liked the social control the CCP possessed, like Tom Friedman or Paul Krugman. The CCP's totalitarianism was what they sought for the US too. The rise of the "progressives" in the Democratic Party share many of the objectives of the CCP and have abandoned the principles of liberal government that have served as our bedrock since 1776.

Consequently, the pro-CCP school has overwhelming support from many in the American elite. There is ample elite support for engagement and far too little for the CCP's destruction. Thus, we conclude that the country needs a new elite, those possessed with the indomitable American spirit of common sense and can-do tenacity, that is able to understand the CCP threat and work to terminate it. We are not optimistic that this will be accomplished easily, but it will be done, as the present divide is unsustainable.

It will be resolved through war, or through the collapse of the "old regime" that is the pro-CCP school. Emphatically, this profound tension will not be resolved through the victory of the pro-CCP school, as the degree to which they are successful in supporting the PRC emboldens the CCP and makes war more likely, and far sooner than is anticipated. This is because the stronger and more secure the CCP are, the more likely they are to achieve their goal of defeating their principal enemy, the United States. This is a goal they possessed well before they came to power in 1949. As we have emphasized, that war will be horrific for all sides, but it will result in the defeat of the CCP abroad and of the pro-CCP school at home.

We are optimistic that the US people will embrace these principles of strategy, marshal its power, cast off the fetters of the pro-CCP school, and move expeditiously to defeat the CCP due to the inherent weakness of their ideology. Manifestly, there must be an immediate reversal to the policies of the Biden administration that are slavishly beholden to the pursuit of unaccountable dialogue with the CCP. The Biden administration's need for "dialogue," to talk to Beijing, betrays the Biden administration's lack of strategic thought.

Fundamentally, the value of strategy is to tell you how to win. Strategy assumes that you have interests to advance and to protect and threats to those interests. The CCP understands this. The CCP considers the US as its foe and acts like it. In a deep sense, the Biden administration is an inmate of the intellectual prison of the pro-CCP school. The Biden administration will not accept that the CCP is the enemy of the US. Thus, it acts like it can alter the CCP's understanding of its interests, which are to defeat the US, and so are inimical to those of the US. The Biden administration will not state the powerful truth: the CCP is the enemy of the US and threatens the national security of the United States in the Indo-Pacific and globally.

At root, this confrontation is zero sum. As Frederick the Great is purported to have stated regarding the origins of the wars over Silesia during the War of Austrian Succession and Seven Years War against Austria's Queen Maria Theresa, "There was no misunderstanding, we both wanted Silesia." So too is it with South China Sea, or Taiwan, hegemony, or whether China or the US will define the political values of the twenty-first century.

The US must possess a strategy for victory. It must behave like the super-power it is. The dialogue so valued by the Biden administration is useful only if conveys one message: you will lose this fight. The struggle with the PRC will define the twenty-first century and will compel the US to employ every tool at its disposal.

In sum, there is a need for renaissance in strategic thought in the US. If there is a silver lining in the Sino-American Cold War, it is that the national security communities have rediscovered the need to possess the understanding of power politics and the principles of strategy. This requires considerable investment to support the necessary changes in JPME, foundations, think tanks, and academic study to cause this rebirth.

A US victory will require many steps, but the most important is the most fundamental: to motivate the American people and their allies to understand, enjoin, and sustain the fight. The rightful possession of confidence in the history and abilities of the United States, and in Western Civilization and the societies the West has created, will serve the aims of explaining and motivating its peoples for the fight. The august history of the United States and the West's unique civilization has demonstrated its effectiveness at sustaining itself and confidence in its political principles and civilization over centuries, even as it now faces new tests. In contrast, its enemy possesses far lower civilization confidence. This is because the CCP is a Western derivative, and its civilization is trapped in a sharp bifurcation between a profound admiration and loathing of the West. The result is that the PRC is fundamentally incoherent and vulnerable to strategies that would capitalize upon its divisions.

A lesson from the British experience in the interwar period is apropos. In two decades, Britain went from the victory of 1918 to the defeat of 1940. With the perspective of history, it is almost as though the US declared a "Ten-Year Rule" as the British did in August 1919. British decision-makers were guided in their defense planning by the assumption that there was not going to be a major war for ten years, and thus kept tight control on defense expenditure. "It should be assumed that the British Empire will not be engaged in any great war during the next ten years, and that no Expeditionary Force is required for this purpose. . . . The principal function of the Military and Air Forces is to provide garrisons for India, Egypt, and new mandated territory and all territories (other than self-governing) under British control."[5] There was no money for military expansion or innovation, combined-arms training, or preparation for future expeditionary warfare.

In the two decades that followed was a crippling freeze on defense spending that was the greatest cause of the British army's lack of modernization and preparation for the Second World War. The British military was to garrison the empire, and from His Majesty's Government's perspective, the war to end all wars had done its job. There was no need to consider or plan for a future one, whether in policy, financial, or military terms. It had a disastrous impact on Britain's domestic arms industry and gave the Treasury (Exchequer) the final decision in considerations of national security. Moreover, it gave a huge disincentive for the War Office to undertake strategic planning or doctrinal development. The rule remained in place, ruinously, until 1932. Britain was unprepared for war in 1939 principally because of its faulty defense planning and financing in the previous two decades.

The march to war in 1939 made General Hastings Ismay, chairman of the military element of the War Cabinet secretariat, angry. "I was not frightened or even excited" at the onset of war, he recalled:

> But I was furious—furious with ourselves as with the Nazis. Less than twenty-one years had passed since the Germans had lain prostrate at our feet. Now they were at our throats. How had we been so craven or careless to allow this to happen? The Cenotaph was almost on the doorsteps of our office, and every time I passed it I felt a sense of guilt that we who had survived the First World War had broken faith with those who had died . . . They had given their lives in the belief that they were fighting the war which was to end all wars. And now their sons and grandsons were about to be sent to the slaughter.[6]

In 1918, Britain had won the war, but lost the peace. Economics and finance trumped strategy and the Exchequer defined the parameters of national security. In similar historical circumstances, in 1991 the United States won the Cold War, and might have enjoyed a century of stability defined by the Pax Americana. Instead, as with Britain, economics and finance bested strategy. Like Britain, the US is on the cusp of losing the peace. Like Britain, it had broken faith with previous generations of Americans. Unlike Britain, the US made a far greater mistake—it actually funded and still funds its peer enemy by allowing PRC entities to raise capital on New York markets.

In essence, the US never had a "ten-year rule" but in a practical sense it possessed something akin to a "thirty-year rule." The US did not lack funds like the British. But like the British, it lacked an understanding of power politics and of imagination. Also like the British, the military increasingly became expeditionary and preparation for great power war went into hibernation during the great Ice Age of US strategic thought from 1993 to today when it arguably remains in a frozen age, albeit perhaps with a mini-thaw evinced in the 2017 National Security Strategy and 2018 Summary of the National Defense Strategy and Nuclear Posture Review.

That the US is in danger of losing the peace won in 1991 is thus not a surprise given its behavior. Prompted by his fury, Ismay's question was how British governments could be so craven or careless to allow the dire situation to develop. That hard and biting question remains relevant today for the American public and the US national security community.

The recognition of the stark failure of the US to prevent the rise of its peer adversary provides the opportunity for a renaissance of strategic thought in the United States. Now that the US faces a peer enemy, it must respond with the energy and focus it did after World War II. That war provided the urgent necessity of applying the principles of power politics to US defense policy. It also necessitated the creation of new intellectual constructs in strategic thought, such as nuclear deterrence theory, and intense study of Russian and Soviet history and of Communist thought.

At present, the strategic intellectual constructs the US needs to combat PRC threat do not require new constructs; the intellectual load today is lighter than in the mid- and late 1940s. What is required is only the rediscovery and application of the wisdom of the previous ages in strategic thought. Just as the renaissance rediscovered the wisdom of classical thought, the renaissance

in US strategic thought we have called for may apply the wisdom of US forefathers as they confronted supreme challenges against a formidable enemy.
There was leadership in the wake of World War II that provided the environ-
ments, such as Rand in its first two decades and the early CIA, to solve the
strategic problems of the early Cold War. Today civilian and military leadership in the US national security community is once again needed to provide
the environment for the rediscovery of power politics and strategy necessary
to defeat the enemy.

Finally, and most importantly, the purpose of this book has been to call
the attention of the American public to the ambition, strategy, and tactics
of the CCP. The CCP intends to destroy the very foundations of the United
States of America through its political warfare tactics, including the ideological assault on the principles and values that our Founders and Framers
assembled some 250 years ago. The notion of individual rights and consent
of the governed is opposed to the CCP's promotion of collectivism and the
authority of the states over the individual. For too long American elites have
either taken this foundation of freedom for granted or have in fact adopted
the tenets of Communism as the most beneficial form of governance. This
is evinced today as the nation is under assault from American Marxists who
seek unhinge the United States from its ideological and institutional foundations, which includes their intent to pack the Supreme Court, add states
to the Union, destroy the border, erode the integrity of the franchise and,
worst of all, the imprisonment of political enemies. American citizens should
understand that the CCP's agenda is aligned with the Communists' agenda
in America.

As an envoi, this book contributes to the overall awakening that is necessary
to save the United States of America at a time of great peril due to ideological
upheaval in its domestic politics while it simultaneously fights the PRC. This
existential foe must be fought in the realms of international politics but also
at home, not only against the PRC's penetration of American institutions,
economy, and society but against its *de facto* allies in the pro-CCP school. In
actuality, the CCP is an illegitimate polity with feet of clay. If Americans can
be united in their understanding of the threat and their confrontation of it,
working with the Chinese people and people of goodwill around the world,

the CCP will fall, as the Soviet Union did. In that manner, the greatest threat to the US and to international peace will be eliminated. Understanding is necessary. Leadership is needed. It is past time to start.

STAY THE COURSE ON CHINA: AN OPEN LETTER TO PRESIDENT TRUMP

Dear President Trump,

Over America's exceptional history, successive generations have risen to the challenge of protecting and furthering our founding principles, and defeating existential threats to our liberties and those of our allies. Today, our generation is challenged to do the same by a virulent and increasingly dangerous threat to human freedoms—the Chinese Communist Party (CCP) through the nation it misrules: the People's Republic of China (PRC).

The Chinese Communists' stated ambitions are antithetical to America's strategic interests, and the PRC is increasingly taking actions that imperil the United States and our allies. The past forty years during which America pursued an open policy of "engagement" with the PRC have contributed materially to the incremental erosion of US national security.

This cannot be permitted to continue.

China is not as we wish it to be. In our political system, politics is the norm, and war is the exception. It is explicitly the opposite in the PRC's worldview. Going forward, we must better understand and deal with this dangerous asymmetry.

We the undersigned, are encouraged by the broad and coherent strategy of robust, alternative policies you have adopted to confront the PRC's campaign to undermine the national interests of the United States and its allies. We encourage you to stay the course on your path of countering Communist China.

We acknowledge and support your robust National Security Strategy that properly sets forth why the United States must counter the PRC. Opposing the advance of tyranny is fully in keeping with the founding principles of America and our rich heritage of defending freedom and liberty, both at home and, where necessary, abroad.

We note the PRC does not recognize the principles and rules of the existing international order, which under a Pax Americana has enabled the greatest period of peace and global prosperity in mankind's history. The PRC rejects this order both ideologically and in practice. China's rulers openly proclaim and insist on a new set of rules to which other nations must conform, such as their efforts to dominate the East and South China Seas and the so-called "Belt and Road Initiative," with its debt-trap diplomacy, designed to extend such hegemony worldwide. The only persistently defining principle of the CCP is the sustainment and expansion of its power.

Over the past forty years of Sino-American relations, many American foreign policy experts did not accurately assess the PRC's intentions or attributed the CCP's reprehensible conduct to the difficulties of governing a country of 1.3 billion people. American policymakers were told time and again by these adherents of the China-engagement school that the PRC would become a "responsible stakeholder" once a sufficient level of economic modernization was achieved. This did not happen and *cannot* so long as the CCP rules China.

The PRC routinely and systematically suppresses religious freedom and free speech, including the imprisonment of over one million citizens in Xinjiang and the growing suppression of Hong Kong's autonomy. The PRC also routinely violates its obligations, as it does with the World Trade Organization, freedom of navigation, and the protection of coral reefs in the South China Sea. Beijing then demands that its own people and the rest of the world accept their false narratives and justifications, demands aptly termed as "Orwellian nonsense."

The PRC is not and never has been a peaceful regime. It uses economic and military force—what it calls its "comprehensive national power"—to bully and intimidate others. The PRC threatens to wage war against a free and democratically led Taiwan.

It is expanding its reach around the globe, co-opting our allies and other nations with the promise of economic gain, often with authoritarian capitalism posing as free commerce, corrupt business practices that go unchecked, state-controlled entities posing as objective academic, scientific or media institutions and trade and development deals that lack reciprocity, transparency and sustainability. The CCP corrupts everything it touches.

This expansionism is not random or ephemeral. It is manifestly the unfolding of the CCP's grand strategy. The Party's ambitions have been given many names, most recently the "China Dream," the "great rejuvenation" of China, or the "Community of Common Destiny." The "Dream" envisioned by the Communist Party is a nightmare for the Chinese people and the rest of the world.

We firmly support the Chinese people, the vast majority of whom want to live peaceful lives.

But we do not support the Communist government of China, nor its control by the dangerous Xi Jinping clique. We welcome the measures you have taken to confront Xi's government and selectively to decouple the US economy from China's insidious efforts to weaken it. No amount of US diplomatic, economic, or military "engagement" will disrupt the CCP's grand strategy.

If there is any sure guide to diplomatic success, it is that when America leads, other nations follow. If history has taught us anything it is that clarity and commitment of leadership in addressing existential threats, like from the PRC, will be followed by our allies when policy prescriptions such as yours become a reality. The PRC's immediate strategy is to delay, stall, and otherwise wait out your presidency. Every effort must be made therefore to institutionalize now the policies and capabilities that can rebalance our economic relations with China, strengthen our alliances with like-minded democracies, and ultimately to defeat the PRC's global ambitions to suppress freedom and liberty. Stay the Course!

Available at: www.jpolrisk.com/stay-the-course-on-china-an-open-letter-to-president-trump

ENDNOTES

Chapter One

1. James Fanell, "Asia Rising: China's Global Naval Strategy and Expanding Force Structure," *Naval War College Review*, Vol. 72, No. 1 (Winter 2019), pp. 33–36. Available at: digital-commons.usnwc.edu/cgi/viewcontent.cgi?article=7871&context=nwc-review. Accessed: July 14, 2023.

2. On the policy of confrontation see, Lianchao Han and Bradley A. Thayer, *Understanding the China Threat* (London: Routledge, 2023); John M. Friend and Bradley A. Thayer, *How China Sees the World: Han-Centrism and the Balance of Power in International Politics* (Lincoln: Potomac Books, 2018). Also see John M. Friend and Bradley A. Thayer, "China's Use of Multilateral Institutions and the US Response: The Need for American Primacy 2.0." in Kai He and Huiyun Feng, eds., *China's Challenges and International Order Transition: Beyond the "Thucydides's Trap"* (Ann Arbor: University of Michigan Press, 2020), pp. 259–279.

3. To maintain this position, US national security decision-makers must recognize that power is the most significant instrument in international politics; and while absolute power is significant, what is more important is the relative power of the state—how it ranks in terms of power against the power of other states. If it chooses to do so, the United States can remain foremost in global politics due to its relative power based on its impressive military, economic, technological, and civilizational capabilities.

Chapter Two

1. Robert B. Strassler, ed., *The Landmark Thucydides: A Comprehensive Guide to the Peloponnesian War* (New York: Free Press, 1996), p. 352.

2. See Lothar Gall, *Bismarck: The White Revolutionary*, vol. 2: 1871–1898 (London: Allen & Unwin, 1986), p. 40; and Erich Eyck, *Bismarck and the German Empire* (New York: George Allen & Unwin, 1950), pp. 187–188.

3. Imanuel Geiss, *German Foreign Policy, 1871–1914* (London: Routledge & Kegan Paul, 1976), p. 26.

4. Bismarck, Dictated note, n.d., in W. N. Medlicott and Dorothy K. Coveney, eds., *Bismarck and Europe* (London: Edward Arnold, 1971), p. 178.

5. For a deeper consideration, see Robert Powell, *In the Shadow of Power: States and Strategies in International Politics* (Princeton, N.J.: Princeton University Press, 1999).

6. Walt submits that the degree of threat is determined by four factors: capabilities, geographic proximity, the offense-defense balance—that is, whether it is easier to take territory (offensive dominance) or defend it (defense dominance)—and indication of aggressive intentions. Prominent works of international relations on the logic of balancing are Stephen M. Walt, *The Origins of Alliances* (Ithaca, N.Y.: Cornell University Press, 1987); and Kenneth N. Waltz, *Man, the State, and War: A Theoretical Analysis* (New York: Columbia University Press, 1959); and Waltz, *Theory of International Politics* (Reading, Mass.: Addison-Wesley, 1979).

7. Although this is unlikely with the PRC as the balance of power discounts ideology, which is a major cause of the PRC's aggression. Other powers like Japan and South Korea are invaluable to the US as well and have major contributions to make. Finally, tripolarity will have its own dynamic, and may be less stable than bipolarity or the classic five European great power multipolarity of eighteenth, nineteenth, and twentieth centuries.

8. This argument is made in Waltz, *Theory of International Politics*; Waltz, "International Structure, National Force, and the Balance of World Power," in James N. Rosenau, ed., *International Politics and Foreign Policy* (New York: Free Press, 1969); and "The Emerging Structure of International Politics," *International Security*, Vol. 18, No. 2 (Fall 1993), pp. 44–79.

9. Jane Perlez and Grace Tatter, "Shared Secrets: How the U.S. and China Worked Together to Spy on the Soviet Union," WBUR "The Great Wager" Podcast, February 18, 2022. Available at: www.wbur.org/hereandnow/2022/02/18/great-wager-spy-soviet-union. Accessed: July 30, 2023.

10. *New York Times* correspondent Patrick Tyler argues that the CIA created a school in Beijing to teach PLA military intelligence how to use the equipment. Monitoring stations in the Mountains of Heaven north of Urumqi in Xinjiang had a good view of Semipalatinsk. These stations were especially valuable to the PRC as they collected signals intelligence on KGB communications, air traffic control, military communications from Soviet Central Asia to East Asia, and Soviet conventional and nuclear forces. In particular, the alert status of Soviet nuclear forces, which would augment the PRC's warning of a Soviet first strike. Patrick Tyler, *A Great Wall: Six Presidents and China an Investigative History* (New York: Century Foundation, 1999), pp. 284–285.

11. Christopher quoted in James Mann, *About Face: A History of America's Curious Relationship with China, from Nixon to Clinton* (New York: Knopf, 1999), p. 109.

12. Mann, *About Face*, p. 111.
13. Mann, *About Face*, pp. 111–112.
14. Han and Thayer, *Understanding the China Threat*, pp. 59–60.
15. On NSDD 11 and 12 see Michael Pillsbury, *The Hundred-Year Marathon: China's Secret Strategy to Replace America as the Global Superpower* (New York: Henry Holt, 2015), p. 73. Pillsbury also notes that Reagan aided the PRC's government-run institutes specializing in "genetic engineer, automation, biotechnology, lasers, space technology, manned spaceflight, intelligent robotics, and more. Reagan even approved a Chinese military delegation visit to one the crown jewels of national security, the Defense Advanced Research Projects Agency." Pillsbury, *The Hundred-Year Marathon*, pp. 73–74.
16. Although US business interests were present in the Soviet Union in the 1920s into the 1930s. During the period the New Economic Policy and in the first Five Year Plan (launched in 1928,) the Soviets purchased and imported foreign production plants, particularly in electrification, tractors, and heavy industry. Foreign experts, especially American, supervised Soviet engineers and workers, setting these plants in operation. Of course, the Soviets were heavily influenced by Frederick Taylor's time-and-motion efficiency (Taylorism) and Henry Ford's mass production techniques (Fordism) and sought American experts to help implement them. For example, International General Electric was heavily involved in the building of the V.I. Lenin hydroelectric plant on the Dnieper modeled on Muscle Shoals hydroelectric plant from 1917–1925, the first unit of the Tennessee Valley Authority. American Hugh Cooper of General Electric was the chief consultant and received the Order of Red Star in 1932, the first foreigner so honored.
17. James Lilley with Jeffrey Lilley, *China Hands: Nine Decades of Adventure, Espionage, and Diplomacy in Asia* (New York: PublicAffairs, 2004), p. 228.
18. Lilley, *China Hands*, p. 229; and Mann, *About Face*, pp. 120–121.
19. Mann notes it was eight alumni, including President Carter himself, who were warmly welcomed by Deng and who noted that "we Chinese will never forget" his role in breaking US relations with Taiwan. Mann, *About Face*, p. 123.
20. "Arms Sales to Taiwan," White House Memorandum for the Record from President Reagan to the Secretary of State George Shultz and Secretary of Defense Caspar Weinberger, 17 August 1982, Declassified 30 August 2019 by National Security Advisor John Bolton. Available at: china.usc.edu/sites/default/files/article/attachments/eagan-1982-08-17-arms-sales-to-taiwan.pdf. Accessed: June 20, 2023.
21. Lilley, *China Hands*, pp. 231–233. Lilley notes a problem that plagued him and that remains present today is that many analysts in CIA "favored a strategic relationship with China over any commitments to Taiwan. In fact . . .

Taiwan was seen as an obstacle if not an albatross to improving relations with the PRC." Lilley, *China Hands*, p. 234.

22. Lilley, *China Hands*, p. 248.

23. Lilley, *China Hands*, p. 248.

24. This was a question others in the Reagan administration were asking as well, including Assistant Secretary of State for East Asia Paul Wolfowitz. Shultz and others argued that Japan should be the principal focus of US diplomacy in Asia as it brought a considerable amount of power to the confrontation with the Soviet Union, in contrast to the PRC. Mann, *About Face*, pp. 128–131.

25. Lilley, *China Hands*, p. 341.

26. Mann, *About Face*, pp. 167–173.

27. Mann, *About Face*, pp. 171–172.

28. Mann, *About Face*, pp. 176–182.

29. These events are well captured in Mann, *About Face*, pp. 179–180.

30. Han and Thayer, *Understanding the China Threat*, pp. 17–73.

31. Mann, *About Face*, p. 183.

32. Bill Keller, "Gorbachev Visits Beijing for Start of Summit Talks," *New York Times*, May 15, 1989. Available at: www.nytimes.com/1989/05/15/world/gorbachev-visits-beijing-for-start-of-summit-talks.html. Accessed: July 9, 2023.

33. Nicholas Kristof, "Hu Yaobang, Ex-Party Chief in China, Dies at 73," *New York Times*, April 16, 1989. Available at: www.nytimes.com/1989/04/16/obituaries/hu-yaobang-ex-party-chief-in-china-dies-at-73.html. Accessed: July 9, 2023.

34. Lilley, *China Hands*, p. 299.

35. Yang and Deng quoted in Lilley, *China Hands*, p. 302.

36. Lilley, *China Hands*, p. 309.

37. Quoted in Lilley, *China Hands*, p. 334.

38. See Barry Naughton, "The Impact of the Tiananmen Crisis on China's Economic Transition," in Jean-Philippe Béja, ed., *The Impact of China's 1989 Tiananmen Massacre* (London: Routledge, 2011), pp. 154–178.

39. Nicholas Kristof, "Deng Is Silent, and the Chinese Can't Tell Where the Power Is," *New York Times*, September 17, 1989. Available at: www.nytimes.com/1989/09/17/weekinreview/the-world-deng-is-silent-and-the-chinese-can-t-tell-where-the-power-is.html. Accessed: July 28, 2023.

40. Lilley, *China Hands*, p. 377.

41. Francis Fukuyama, "The End of History?" *The National Interest*, No. 16 (Summer 1989), pp. 3–18, 3. Emphasis original.

42. Fukuyama, "The End of History?" p. 3.

43. As President Clinton stated: "Ultimately, the best strategy to ensure our security and to build durable peace is to support the advance of democracy elsewhere. Democracies don't attack each other." President Bill Clinton, State of

the Union Address, January 25 1994 (Washington D.C., 1994). This strategy was advanced in the Clinton administration's 1994 *National Security Strategy of Engagement and Enlargement*. National Security Advisor Anthony Lake summarized the reasoning in a speech at Johns Hopkins University on September 21, 1993: "First, we should strengthen the community of major market democracies—including our own—which constitutes the core from which enlargement is proceeding." Second, "we should help foster and consolidate new democracies and market economies, where possible, especially in states of special significance and opportunity." Third, "we must counter the aggression—and support the liberalization—of states hostile to democracy and markets." Fourth and finally, "we need to pursue our humanitarian agenda not only by providing aid, but also by working to help democracy and market economics take root in regions of greatest humanitarian concern."

44. As experienced by one of the authors' completion of Joint Professional Military Education (JPME) Phase I in 1999.

45. While economics is fundamental as the economy is the locomotive of a state's power, we recognize that other factors, importantly innovation and technological development, military effectiveness, and natural and human resources are relevant as well.

46. The final draft, which was substantially revised on these points, was released in April 1992.

47. In 1994, Clinton separated, or de-linked, human rights considerations from the annual MFN renewal, but the annual decision was still required. In fact, a waiver was required each year since 1980 for the PRC have MFN, and each year it was provided. Permanent MFN, or Normal Trade Status (NTS), for the PRC was signed into law in October 2000, pending the PRC's accession to the WTO. As WTO accession did not occur until December 2001, in June 2001, President Bush approved the final waiver, as did Congress.

48. Mann, *About Face*, pp. 231–233; and pp. 279–283.

49. Mann, *About Face*, p. 282. Another exceptional account of these negotiations is Larry M. Wortzel, "Missionary Zeal, Profits, and Constituent Interests," in Shiping Hua, ed., *The Political Logic of the U.S.-China Trade War* (Lanham, MD: Lexington Books, 2022), pp. 171–192.

50. Mann, *About Face*, p. 283.

51. Mann, *About Face*, pp. 283–284.

52. Mann, *About Face*, pp. 284–285.

53. Mann, *About Face*, pp. 284–285.

54. Mann, *About Face*, p. 285.

55. Mann, *About Face*, pp. 285–288.

56. Mann, *About Face*, pp. 294–296.

57. The legislation establishing PNTR established a Congressional-Executive Commission on China (CECC) comprised of nine senators, nine

representatives, appointed by the House and Senate leadership, representative of the Departments of State, Commerce, and Labor, and two representatives appointed by the president. Its legislative mandate is to monitor human rights, the development of the rule of law in China, maintain a database of political prisoners as well as persons detained or imprisoned by the PRC's government for exercising their human rights, and submit an annual report to Congress and the president. Separate legislation established the United States-China Economic and Security Review Commission (USCC, originally United States-China Security Review Commission). USCC is charged with monitoring and investigate the national security implications of the bilateral trade and economic relationship as well as the PRC's compliance with the WTO and reports annually to Congress. See Wortzel, "Missionary Zeal, Profits, and Constituent Interests," pp. 173–174.

58. Mann, *About Face*, p. 295.

59. Mann, *About Face*, pp. 310–314.

60. Mann, *About Face*, pp. 329–331.

61. Transcript of President Bill Clinton's press conference with Jiang Zemin, January 28, 1997. Also see James Mann, "U.S.-China Relationship: Economics and Security in Perspective," written testimony before the U.S.-China Economic and Security Review Commission hearing, February 1, 2007. Available at: www.uscc.gov/sites/default/files/2.1.2007mann_james_statement.pdf. Accessed: August 11, 2023.

62. Remarks by Bill Clinton to the Johns Hopkins University, Paul H. Nitze School of Advanced International Studies, March 8, 2000.

63. John Mintz, "Missile Failures Led to Loral-China Link," *Washington Post*, June 12, 1998. Available at: www.washingtonpost.com/wp-srv/politics/special/campfin/stories/rocket061298.htm. Accessed: September 1, 2023.

64. Jonathan Peterson, "Clinton Was Warned Against China Launch," *Los Angeles Times*, 23 May 23, 1998. Available at: www.latimes.com/archives/la-xpm-1998-may-23-mn-52739-story.html. Accessed: September 1, 2023.

65. "Campaign Finance Key Player: John Huang," *Washington Post*, July 24, 1997, www.washingtonpost.com/wp-srv/politics/special/campfin/players/huang.html. Accessed: September 1, 2023.

66. There were other nonofficial measures that were taken in the 1990s. Several of the interviews we conducted noted that James Lilley, former National Intelligence Office on China and Director of the American Institute in Taiwan, former Ambassador in Beijing, and Assistant Secretary of Defense for International Security Affairs, ran annual conferences and "Red" and "Blue" team exercises on the strategic objectives of the People's Liberation Army. See Lilley, *China Hands*.

67. Governor George W. Bush, "A Distinctly American Internationalism," speech

at the Ronald Reagan Presidential Library, Simi Valley, Calif., November 19, 1999.

68. The George W. Bush administration did advance discussion of major arms sales to Taiwan. But 9/11, as discussed below, and the fact that the DPP did not yet have its political sea legs in its first time in office, and domestic opposition in the US hindered this. Email communication with former official in the Reagan and George H.W. Bush administrations, August 10, 2023.

69. Robert B. Zoellick, "Whither China? From Membership to Responsibility," Remarks to National Committee on U.S.–China Relations, New York City, NY, September 21, 2005.

70. U.S. Department of Defense, *Quadrennial Defense Review Report* (Washington, D.C.: Department of Defense, 2006), p. 29.

71. Bradley A. Thayer, "While the U.S. Wasn't Watching, China Became the Strategic Beneficiary of 9/11," *The Hill*, March 8, 2019. Available at: thehill.com/opinion/international/431620-while-the-us-wasnt-watching-china-became-strategic-beneficiary-of-9–11. Accessed: April 30, 2023.

72. 新华社，江泽民的大智慧抓住了20年战略机遇期，新华社，2020年07月21日。Available at: cn3.uscnpm.org/model_item.html?action=view&table=article&id=22428. Accessed: December 19, 2022.

73. The development and opportunity provided by the BRI is well captured in Kent E. Calder's *Super Continent: The Logic of Eurasian Integration* (Stanford: Stanford University Press, 2019).

74. President Barack Obama, "Remarks by the President at Cairo University, 6–04-09," Cairo University, June 4, 2009. Available at: obamawhitehouse.archives.gov/the-press-office/remarks-president-cairo-university-6–04-09. Accessed: May 4, 2023.

75. "America does not presume to know what is best for everyone, just as we would not presume to pick the outcome of a peaceful election. But I do have an unyielding belief that all people yearn for certain things: the ability to speak your mind and have a say in how you are governed; confidence in the rule of law and the equal administration of justice; government that is transparent and doesn't steal from the people; the freedom to live as you choose. These are not just American ideas; they are human rights. And that is why we will support them everywhere . . . . government of the people and by the people sets a single standard for all who would hold power: You must maintain your power through consent, not coercion; you must respect the rights of minorities, and participate with a spirit of tolerance and compromise; you must place the interests of your people and the legitimate workings of the political process above your party." Obama, "Remarks by the President at Cairo University, 6–04-09."

76. President Barack Obama, "Remarks by President Obama to the Australia Parliament," Canberra, Australia, November 17, 2011. Available at:

obamawhitehouse.archives.gov/the-press-office/2011/11/17/remarks-president
-obama-australian-parliament. Accessed: May 4, 2023.

77. For more on the PRC's maritime escalation at Scarborough Shoal in 2012
    see Ryan D. Martinson, *Echelon Defense: The Role of Sea Power in Chinese
    Maritime Dispute Strategy*, U.S. Naval War College, China Maritime Studies
    Institute Red Books, Study No. 15, (2018). Available at: digital-commons.
    usnwc.edu/cgi/viewcontent.cgi?article=1014&context=cmsi-red-books.
    Accessed: August 28, 2023.

78. Fanell, "Asia Rising," p. 20.

79. Dzirhan Mahadzir, "VIDEO: China Coast Guard Blast Philippine Military
    Resupply with Water Cannons," *USNI News*, August 7, 2023. Available at: news.
    usni.org/2023/08/07/video-china-coast-guard-blast-philippine-military
    -resupply-with-water-canons. Accessed: August 28, 2023.

80. Mutual Defense Treaty between the Republic of the Philippines and the
    United States of America. Signed in Washington, D.C., August 30, 1951.
    Available at: www.officialgazette.gov.ph/1951/08/30/mutual-defense-treaty
    -between-the-republic-of-the-philippines-and-the-united-states-of-america
    -august-30–1951. Accessed: August 12, 2023.

81. For specific details on what the PRC built in the Spratly Islands starting
    in 2013, see the CSIS Asia Maritime Transparency Initiative "China Island
    Tracker." Available at: amti.csis.org/island-tracker/china. Accessed: August
    13, 2023.

82. Quoted in Ryo Nakamura, "U.S. and Philippines Rapidly Draw Near to
    Counter China," *Nikkei*, May 2, 2023. Available at: asia.nikkei.com/Politics
    /International-relations/U.S.-and-Philippines-rapidly-draw-near-to-counter
    -China. Accessed: May 2, 2023.

83. United States Secretary of State Michael R. Pompeo, "Communist China and
    the Free World's Future," Remarks at the Richard Nixon Presidential Library
    and Museum, July 23, 2020. Available at: sv.usembassy.gov/secretary-michael
    -r-pompeo-remarks-at-the-richard-nixon-presidential-library-and-museum
    -communist-china-and-the-free-worlds-future. Accessed: August 31, 2023.

84. Pompeo, "Communist China and the Free World's Future."

85. These documents were the NSS, the unclassified summary of the *National
    Defense Strategy*, and the *Nuclear Posture Review*.

86. James E. Fanell and Bradley A. Thayer, "The Great Restoration: The Return
    to Engagement with Communist China," *American Greatness*, September
    25, 2023. Available at: amgreatness.com/2023/09/25/the-great-restoration-
    the-return-to-engagement-with-communist-china. Accessed: September 25,
    2023.

87. These remarks were echoed by his successor, Jiang Zemin, who made the
    promise that China would never to seek hegemony in a speech at Cambridge
    University in 1999. Hu Jintao, Jiang's successor, not only repeated the rhetoric

of not seeking hegemony but also added "never engage in expansion," in a keynote speech at China's 2008 Boao Forum for Asia Annual Conference.

88. Xu Jian, "Rethinking China's Period of Strategic Opportunity," *China International Studies* (March/April 2014), pp. 51–70. Available at: www.ciis .org.cn/english/2014–05/28/content_6942258.htm. Accessed: January 19, 2023.

89. See James Mann, *The China Fantasy: Why Capitalism Will Not Bring Democracy to China* (New York: Viking Penguin, 2007); and Stewart Paterson, *China, Trade and Power: Why the West's Economic Engagement Has Failed* (London: London Publishing Partnership, 2018).

90. Hu Jintao address to APEC CEO conference, November 19, 2005.

91. Bradley A. Thayer and Lianchao Han, "Our Real Problem with China: Xi Jinping," *The Spectator*, May 10, 2019. Available at: spectator.us/problem -china-xi-jinping. Accessed: April 19, 2023.

92. Paterson, *China, Trade and Power*, p. 12.

93. Paterson, *China, Trade and Power*, p. 12.

94. Paterson, *China, Trade and Power*, p. 12.

95. Paterson, *China, Trade and Power*, p. 141.

96. This is a major argument of Paterson in *China, Trade and Power*.

97. Mann, *The China Fantasy*, pp. 103–104.

98. Mann, *The China Fantasy*, pp. 104–105.

99. Paterson, *China, Trade and Power*, p. 148.

100. Ben Westcott, "Chinese media calls for 'people's war' as US trade war heats up", *New York Times*, May 14, 2019. www.edition.cnn.com/2019/05/14 /asia/china-us-beijing-propaganda-intl/index.html.

101. Department of Homeland Security, "DHS Warns American Businesses about Data Services and Equipment from Firms Linked to Chinese Government," 22 December 2020. Available at: www.dhs.gov/news/2020/12/22/dhs-warns -american-businesses-about-data-services-and-equipment-firms-linked -chinese. Accessed: July 1, 2023.

102. National Counterintelligence and Security Center, "Safeguarding Our Future: U.S. Business Risk: People's Republic of China (PRC) Laws Expands Beijing's Oversight of Foreign and Domestic Companies," 20 June 2023. Available at: www.dni.gov/files/NCSC/documents/SafeguardingOurFuture /FINAL_NCSC_SOF_Bulletin_PRC_Laws.pdf. Accessed: July 10, 2023.

Chapter Three

1. James Carafano, "Robert Gates: 21st Century Cold Warrior," The Heritage Foundation, August 4, 2009. Available at: www.heritage.org/defense /commentary/robert-gates-21st-century-cold-warrior. Accessed: July 15, 2023.

2. John B. Hattendorf, *The Evolution of the U.S. Navy's Maritime Strategy*,

Newport Papers No. 20 (2004). Available at: digital-commons.usnwc.edu /usnwc-newport-papers/20. Accessed: September 2, 2023.

3.   Nye first developed the concept of soft power a generation ago in Joseph S. Nye, Jr., *Bound to Lead: The Changing Nature of American Power* (New York: Basic Books, 1991); and more fully developed the concept in his *Soft Power: The Means to Success in World Politics* (New York: Public Affairs, 2005).

4.   For more on Confucius Institutes see Lee Edwards, "Confucius Institutes: China's Trojan Horse," *Heritage Foundation*, May 27, 2021. Available at: www.heritage.org/homeland-security/commentary/confucius-institutes -chinas-trojan-horse. Accessed: July 12, 2023.

5.   An outstanding case was the 2004 Boxing Day earthquake and tsunami, which occurred in the Indian Ocean near Sumatra and killed some 300,000 people. The United States was the first to respond with the immediate dispatch of the US Navy's *Abraham Lincoln* Carrier Strike Group to lead rescue and recovery operations, followed by the *Bonhomme Richard* Expeditionary Strike Group. Washington rapidly followed up with Operation Unified Assistances, a large contribution of aid and deployed the US military to South and Southeast Asia for many months to help with the aftermath of the disaster. About 20,000 US soldiers, sailors, airmen, and marines responded by providing water, food, medical aid, disease treatment and prevention as well as forensic assistance to help identify the bodies of those killed. Only the US military could have accomplished this Herculean effort. No other state or international organization possesses the communications capabilities or global logistical reach of the US military. The PRC duly noted the US success, and that accounts for their development of similar capabilities, such as the *Peace Ark* Type 920 hospital ship to match USNS *Comfort* and *Mercy* as well is their aircraft carrier force, now consisting of three flat-tops.

6.   See Colin S. Gray, *Schools for Strategy: Teaching Strategy for 21ˢᵗ Century Conflict* (Carlisle, PA: Strategic Studies Institute, U.S. Army War College, 2009), pp. 40–51.

7.   Carl von Clausewitz, *On War*, edited and translated by Michael Howard and Peter Paret (Princeton, N.J.: Princeton University Press, 1976), p. 141.

8.   Quoted in Correlli Barnett, *The Swordbearers: Studies in Supreme in the First World War* (London: Eyre and Spottiswoode, 1953), p. 195.

9.   See Bradley A. Thayer, "Colin Gray and Strategic Thought," *Comparative Strategy*, Vol. 40, No. 2 (2021), pp. 128–132.

10. Colin S. Gray, *Strategy and History: Essays on Theory and Practice* (New York: Routledge, 2006), pp. 51–53 and pp. 78–79.

11. Gray, *History and Strategy*, p. 51; and Thayer, "Colin Gray and Strategic Thought," pp. 128–132.

12. von Clausewitz, *On War*, pp. 119–121. In Chinese strategic thought, there

is an absence of a sensitivity to friction. This is one more cause of concern in the intensifying Sino-American Cold War.

13. Gray, *Schools for Strategy*, pp. 40–51.

14. Quoted in Andrew F. Krepinevich and Barry D. Watts, *The Last Warrior: Andrew Marshall and the Shaping of Modern American Defense Strategy* (New York: Basic Books, 2015), p. 247.

15. Interview with Colonel Grant Newsham, US Marine Corps (Retired), September 10, 2023.

16. A good comparison is with pilot training and continuing education. Many people are trained, and once one becomes a pilot, education and training do not stop, but in the course of their careers are re-trained and certified, and very senior instructor pilots serve to educate and mentor juniors. This has contributed to great safety and performance in the US airline industry.

17. Colin S. Gray, *The Strategy Bridge: Theory for Practice* (New York: Oxford University Press, 2010).

18. In World War II, President Franklin Roosevelt and the Joint Chiefs of Staff were confident that the United States would win the long war against the Germans, Japanese, and Italians, for sound reasons: the central tenet of the allied victory was superiority in manufacturing of the material—and through training, the men—necessary for victory. Naturally, confidence cannot be misplaced, and, indeed, will not be if it is anchored on a clear understanding of strengths and advantages in the possession of the United States, and knowledge of US weaknesses. On the other side of the coin, US decision-makers must have awareness of the rival's strengths and weaknesses, and a strategy to have that competition—ideally—in an arena of the US's strength versus opponent's weakness.

19. RADM Edwin T. Layton, USN (Ret.), *And I Was There: Pearl Harbor and Midway—Breaking the Secrets* (New York: William Morrow, 1985), p. 438.

20. Charles Richard, former Commander, US Strategic Command, "Virtual Event: A Conversation with Admiral Richard," Hudson Institute, August 26, 2021. Available at: s3.amazonaws.com/media.hudson.org/Transcript-%20 A%20Conversation%20with%20Admiral%20Richard.pdf. Accessed: July 10, 2023.

21. John Koht, "Yang Reportedly Says Carrier to Be Purchased," *South China Morning Post*, December 14, 1992, p. 10. Accessed: July 24, 2023.

22. Koht, "Yang Reportedly Says Carrier to Be Purchased."

23. William C. Triplett II, ""Inside China's Scary New Military-Industrial Complex," *Washington Post*, May 8, 1994. Available at: www.washington-post.com/archive/1994/05/08/inside-chinas-scary-new-military-industrial-complex/24d132d0-a7aa-453f-bd11-cd87c938ced3. Accessed: August 18, 2023.

24. Interview with Triplett, August 15, 2023.

25. Richard Fisher, "10 Years of Illegal China-North Korea Nuclear Missile Cooperation," *Epoch Times*, April 15, 2022. Available at: www.theepoch times.com/10-years-of-illegal-china-north-korea-nuclear-missile-cooperation _4406600.html?slsuccess=1. Accessed: September 5, 2023.

26. H.I. Sutton, "North Korea's New Submarine Carries 10 Nuclear Missiles," *Naval News*, September 8, 2023. Available at: www.navalnews.com/naval -news/2023/09/north-koreas-new-submarine-carries-10-nuclear-missiles. Accessed: September 5, 2023.

27. Remarks taken from interview with Rick Fisher, September 8, 2023.

28. Bill Gertz, *Breakdown: How America's Intelligence Failures Led to September 11* (Washington, D.C.: Regnery Publishing, 2002), p.73.

29. Gertz, *Breakdown*, p. 74

30. Gertz, *Breakdown*, p. 75.

31. James E. Fanell, "China's Global Navy—Today's Challenge for the United States and the U.S. Navy," *Naval War College Review*, Vol. 73, No. 4 (Autumn 2020), p. 26.

32. Interview response from Newsham, September 10, 2023.

33. James Fanell and Bradley Thayer, "We Need a New 'Admirals' Revolt,'" *American Greatness*, June 25, 2023. Available at: amgreatness. com/2023/06/25/we-need-a-new-admirals-revolt. Accessed: June 25, 2023.

34. "China Naval Modernization: Implications for U.S. Navy Capabilities— Background and Issues for Congress," RL33153, *Congressional Research Service*, Updated 19 October 2023, p. 9. Available at: crsreports.congress. gov/product/pdf/RL/RL33153/275. Accessed: December 20, 2023.

35. China Naval Modernization: Implications for U.S. Navy Capabilities— Background and Issues for Congress," p. 9.

36. Edward Timberlake and William C. Triplett II, *Red Dragon Rising: Communist China's Military Threat to America* (Washington, D.C.: Regnery, Publishing, 2002), p. 133.

37. William C. Triplett II, "Dangerous Embrace," *New York Times*, September 10, 1994, Available at: www.nytimes.com/1994/09/10/opinion/dangerous -embrace.html?searchResultPosition=167. Accessed: July 10, 2023.

38. Interview with Triplett, August 15, 2023.

39. Interview with Triplett, August 15, 2023.

40. Interview with Triplett, August 15, 2023.

41. Caitlin Campbell, "China Primer: U.S.-China Military-to-Military Relations," Congressional Research Service, January 4, 2021. Available at: crsreports.congress.gov/product/pdf/IF/IF11712. Accessed: July 31, 2023.

42. Interview with Triplett, August 15, 2023.

43. One of the author's eye-witness observations aboard the USS *Kitty Hawk* in the port of Hong Kong February 5, 2005.

44. David Lague, "U.S. Commander Given Tour by Chinese Military," *New York*

Times, August 21, 2007. Available at: www.nytimes.com/2007/08/21/world /asia/21cnd-china.html. Accessed: July 10, 2023.

45. "Freedom of Navigation Patrols May End 'In Disaster': Chinese Admiral," *Reuters*, July 18, 2016. Available at: www.reuters.com/news/picture/freedom-of-navigation-patrols-may-end-in-idUSKCN0ZY0FJ. Accessed: August 11, 2023.

46. James Fanell, "Stop 'Engagement at All Costs,'" USNI *Proceedings*, September 2016, p. 10.

47. Fanell, "Stop 'Engagement at All Costs,'" p. 10.

48. Bill Owens, "America Must Start Treating China as a Friend," *Financial Times*, November 17, 2009. Available at: www.ft.com/content/69241506-d3b2-11de-8caf-00144feabdc0. Accessed: September 7, 2023.

49. Bill Gertz and Rowan Scarborough, "Inside the Ring: Abandoning Taiwan," *Washington Times*, July 30, 1999, p. A11. The authors also acknowledge that Admiral Blair attempted to defend those comments a decade later when testifying before the Senate for his nomination by President Obama for the position of Director of National Intelligence; see William Lowther, "U.S.' Blair defends 'turd' comment, Taiwan record," *Taipei Times*, February 19, 2000. Available at: www.taipeitimes.com/News/taiwan/archives/2009/02/01/2003434953. Accessed: September 5, 2023.

50. Nick Schifrin and Dan Sagalyn, "Indo-Pacific Commander Discusses Rising Tensions with China, Future of the Region," *PBS News Hour*, December 15, 2022. Available at: www.pbs.org/newshour/show/pacific-commander-of-u-s -navy-discusses-rising-tensions-with-china-future-of-region. Accessed: July 5, 2023.

51. *Chief of Naval Operations: Navigation Plan 2022*, United States Navy, Chief of Naval Operations, 26 July 2022, p. 3. Available at: www.dvidshub.net /publication/issues/64582. Accessed: September 10, 2023.

52. *Chief of Naval Operations: Navigation Plan 2022*, p. 3.

53. *United States Statutes at Large*, 1939–41, Vol. 54, Part 1 (Washington, D.C.: Government Printing Office, 1941), pp. 394–396. Available at: www.history. navy.mil/browse-by-topic/wars-conflicts-and-operations/world-war-ii/1941 /prelude/naval-expansion-act-14-june-1940.html. Accessed: September 10, 2023.

54. "Military Must Focus on Current Wars, Gates Says," *NBC News/Associated Press*, May 13, 2008. Available at: www.nbcnews.com/id/wbna24600218. Accessed: May 1, 2023.

55. See "Military Must Focus on Current Wars, Gates Says."

56. For Adm. Fallon's comments, see "Chinese Invited to Watch US Exercises Off Guam," New York Times, May 15, 2006. Available at: www.nytimes. com/2006/05/15/world/asia/15iht-games.html. Accessed: September 12, 2023. Adm. Keating's comments are quoted in Al Pessin, "US Commander

Calls Chinese Interest in Aircraft Carriers 'Understandable,'" Voice of America, May 12, 2007, available at: www.voanews.com/a/a-13-2007-05 -12-voa5/332480.html. Accessed: September 12, 2023.

57. Trevor N. Dupuy, *A Genius for War: The German Army and General Staff, 1807–1945* (Fairfax, VA: Hero Books, 1977).

58. Documenting the scope of this penetration as well as advancing solutions to end it is Frank Gaffney, with Dede Laugesen, *The Indictment: Prosecuting the China Communist Party and Friends for Crimes Against America, China, and the World* (New York: Skyhorse Publishing, 2023).

59. Interview with Newsham, September 10, 2023.

60. M. Taylor Fravel, J. Stapleton Roy, Michael D. Swaine, Susan A. Thornton, and Ezra Vogel, "Making China a U.S. Enemy Is Counterproductive," *Washington Post*, July 3, 2019. Available at: www.washingtonpost.com/opinions /making-china-a-us-enemy-is-counterproductive/2019/07/02/647d49d0– 9bfa-11e9-b27f-ed2942f73d70_story.html. Accessed: September 4, 2023.

61. Fravel, Roy, Swaine, Thornton, and Vogel, "Making China a U.S. Enemy Is Counterproductive."

62. Fravel, Roy, Swaine, Thornton, and Vogel, "Making China a U.S. Enemy Is Counterproductive."

63. The response to this pro-PRC letter was the publication of the "Stay the Course on China: An Open Letter to President Trump" published two weeks later, July 18, 2019, in the *Journal of Political Risk*. Available at: www.jpolrisk. com/stay-the-course-on-china-an-open-letter-to-president-trump. Accessed: September 4, 2023. This letter was signed by over 130 American patriots from across the country. And in an example of how the PRC seeks to silence or punish those who speak out against the PRC, the PRC foreign ministry criticized the "Stay the Course on China" letter during its regular press conference of July 22, 2019. The criticism was featured on the important news column on *Xinhua*'s home page. The article's title is "Ministry of Foreign Affairs: U.S. Anti-China Open Letter Cannot Dictate the Direction of Sino-U.S. Relations" (外交部：美反华公开信左右不了中美关系前进方向). Available at: www.xinhuanet.com/world/2019–07/22/c_1124784885. htm. Accessed: September 4, 2023. When asked about the letter, PRC MFA spokesman Geng Shuang said that the "so-called open letter is full of ideological prejudice and Cold War zero-sum thinking; smears domestic and foreign policy in every conceivable way; vigorously incites the Sino-US conflict; and contains ill-founded content. The letter's signers even include Falun Gong cultists, which greatly compromises the seriousness of the open letter."

Chapter Four

1. A nautical term meaning to be confused, or to lose track of what is occurring. Nautical sextants have a bubble that must be kept level to make a proper

sighting. "Losing the bubble" means that you had no reference to level and have lost the fix. In this context it means losing sight of the threat of the PRC.

2.   Kate O'Keeffe and Aruna Viswanatha, "A DuPont China Deal Reveals Cracks in U.S. National-Security Screening", *Wall Street Journal*, August 12, 2023. Available at: www.wsj.com/articles/a-dupont-china-deal-reveals -cracks-in-u-s-national-security-screening-665cb50c?st=23ezcvp2w-b3l57r&reflink=article_email_share. Accessed: August 12, 2023.

3.   Interview with Charles Kupperman, former Deputy National Security Advisor to President Trump, August 8, 2023.

4.   Han and Thayer, *Understanding the China Threat*, pp. 163–186.

Chapter Five

1.   Quoted in Warren I. Cohen, *America's Response to China*, 4th ed. (New York: Columbia University Press, 1990), p. 179.

2.   We would add that while the PRC on was on the path to democracy, many were not reticent about making money hand over fist, thus profiting from the PRC's rise.

3.   Gina Raimondo, "U.S. Secretary of Commerce Gina Raimondo Delivers Remarks Ahead of Bilateral Meeting with PRC Minister of Commerce Wang Wentao," U.S. Commerce Department, 28 August 2023, Available at: www.commerce.gov/news/speeches/2023/08/us-secretary-commerce-gina -raimondo-delivers-remarks-ahead-bilateral-meeting. Accessed: August 30, 2023.

4.   Joseph R. Biden, "Remarks by President Biden in a Press Conference," White House, 10 September 2023. Available at: www.whitehouse.gov/brief-ing-room/speeches-remarks/2023/09/10/remarks-by-president-biden-in-a-press-conference-2/. Accessed: September 1, 2023.

5.   United Kingdom, The National Archives, CAB 23/15/616A, dated August 15, 1919, p. 1. Available at: filestore.nationalarchives.gov.uk/pdfs/small/cab -23–15-wc-616a.pdf. Accessed: September 1, 2023.

6.   Lord Ismay, *The Memoirs of General Lord Ismay* (New York: Viking Press, 1960), p. 99.

BIBLIOGRAPHY

Barnett, Correlli, *The Swordbearers: Studies in Supreme in the First World War* (London: Eyre and Spottiswoode, 1953).

Biden, Joseph R., "Remarks by President Biden in a Press Conference," White House, 10 September 2023. Available at: www.whitehouse.gov/briefing -room/speeches-remarks/2023/09/10/remarks-by-president-biden-in -a-press-conference-2

Bush, Governor George W., "A Distinctly American Internationalism," speech at the Ronald Reagan Presidential Library, Simi Valley, Calif., November 19, 1999.

Calder, Kent E., *Super Continent: The Logic of Eurasian Integration* (Stanford: Stanford University Press, 2019).

"Campaign Finance Key Player: John Huang," *Washington Post*, July 24, 1997. Available at: www.washingtonpost.com/wp-srv/politics/special/campfin /players/huang.htm

Campbell, Caitlin, "China Primer: U.S.-China Military-to-Military Relations," Congressional Research Service, January 4, 2021. Available at: crsreports.congress.gov/product/pdf/IF/IF11712

Carafano, James, "Robert Gates: 21st Century Cold Warrior," Heritage Foundation, August 4, 2009. Available at: www.heritage.org/defense /commentary/robert-gates-21st-century-cold-warrior

Chief of Naval Operations: Navigation Plan 2022, United States Navy, Chief of Naval Operations, 26 July 2022. Available at: www.dvidshub.net /publication/issues/64582

China Naval Modernization: Implications for U.S. Navy Capabilities— Background and Issues for Congress," RL33153, *Congressional Research*

Service, Updated 19 October 2023. Available at: www.crsreports.congress. gov/product/pdf/RL/RL33153/275

Clinton, President Bill, Remarks by Bill Clinton to the Johns Hopkins University, Paul H. Nitze School of Advanced International Studies, March 8, 2000.

Clinton, President Bill, *State of the Union Address, January 25, 1994* (Washington D.C., 1994).

Cohen, Warren I., *America's Response to China*, 4th ed. (New York: Columbia University Press, 1990).

CSIS Asia Maritime Transparency Initiative "China Island Tracker." Available at: amti.csis.org/island-tracker/china

Department of Homeland Security, "DHS Warns American Businesses about Data Services and Equipment from Firms Linked to Chinese Government," 22 December 2020. Available at: dhs.gov/news/2020/12/22/dhs-warns -american-businesses-about-data-services-and-equipment-firms-linked -chinese

Dupuy, Trevor N., *A Genius for War: The German Army and General Staff, 1807–1945* (Fairfax, VA: Hero Books, 1977).

Edwards, Lee, "Confucius Institutes: China's Trojan Horse," Heritage Foundation, May 27, 2021. Available at: www.heritage.org/homeland -security/commentary/confucius-institutes-chinas-trojan-horse

Eyck, Erich, *Bismarck and the German Empire* (New York: George Allen & Unwin, 1950).

Fanell, James E., "Asia Rising: China's Global Naval Strategy and Expanding Force Structure," *Naval War College Review*, Vol. 72, No. 1 (Winter 2019), pp. 33–36. Available at: digital-commons.usnwc.edu/cgi/viewcontent.cgi ?article=7871&context=nwc-review

Fanell, James E., "China's Global Navy—Today's Challenge for the United States and the U.S. Navy," *Naval War College Review*, Vol. 73, No. 4 (Autumn 2020).

Fanell, James E., "Stop 'Engagement at All Costs,'" USNI *Proceedings*, September 2016.

Fanell, James E., and Bradley A. Thayer, "The Great Restoration: The Return to Engagement with Communist China," *American Greatness*,

September 25, 2023. Available at: amgreatness.com/2023/09/25/the-great -restoration-the-return-to-engagement-with-communist-china

Fanell, James E., and Bradley A. Thayer, "We Need a New 'Admirals' Revolt,'" *American Greatness*, June 25, 2023. Available at: amgreatness.com/2023 /06/25/we-need-a-new-admirals-revolt

Fisher, Richard, "10 Years of Illegal China-North Korea Nuclear Missile Cooperation," *Epoch Times*, April 15, 2022. Available at: theepochtimes. com/10-years-of-illegal-china-north-korea-nuclear-missile-cooperation _4406600.html?slsuccess=1

Fravel, M. Taylor, J. Stapleton Roy, Michael D. Swaine, Susan A. Thornton, and Ezra Vogel, "Making China a U.S. Enemy Is Counterproductive," *Washington Post*, July 3, 2019. Available at:washingtonpost.com/opinions /making-china-a-us-enemy-is-counterproductive/2019/07/02 /647d49d0–9bfa-11e9-b27f-ed2942f73d70_story.html

"Freedom of Navigation Patrols May End 'In Disaster': Chinese Admiral," *Reuters*, July 18, 2016. Available at: reuters.com/news/picture/freedom-of -navigation-patrols-may-end-in-idUSKCN0ZY0FJ

Friend, John M., and Bradley A. Thayer, "China's Use of Multilateral Institutions and the U.S. Response: The Need for American Primacy 2.0." in Kai He and Huiyun Feng, eds., *China's Challenges and International Order Transition: Beyond the "Thucydides's Trap"* (Ann Arbor: University of Michigan Press, 2020), pp. 259–279.

Friend, John M., and Bradley A. Thayer, *How China Sees the World: Han-Centrism and the Balance of Power in International Politics* (Lincoln: Potomac Books, 2018).

Fukuyama, Francis, "The End of History?" *The National Interest*, No. 16 (Summer 1989), pp. 3–18.

Gaffney, Frank, *The Indictment: Prosecuting the China Communist Party and Friends for Crimes Against America, China, and the World* (New York: Skyhorse Publishing, 2023).

Gall, Lothar, *Bismarck: The White Revolutionary*, vol. 2: 1871–1898 (London: Allen & Unwin, 1986).

Geiss, Imanuel, *German Foreign Policy, 1871–1914* (London: Routledge & Kegan Paul, 1976).

Gertz, Bill, *Breakdown: How America's Intelligence Failures Led to September 11* (Washington, D.C.: Regnery Publishing, 2002).

Gertz, Bill, "Panel Finds CIA soft on China," *Washington Times*, July 6, 2001. Available at: washingtontimes.com/news/2001/jul/6/20010706–024147 -1037r

Gertz, Bill, and Rowan Scarborough, "Inside the Ring: Abandoning Taiwan," *Washington Times*, July 30, 1999, p. A11.

Gray, Colin S., *Schools for Strategy: Teaching Strategy for 21st Century Conflict* (Carlisle, PA: Strategic Studies Institute, U.S. Army War College, 2009).

Gray, Colin S., *Strategy and History: Essays on Theory and Practice* (New York: Routledge, 2006).

Gray, Colin S., *The Strategy Bridge: Theory for Practice* (New York: Oxford University Press, 2010).

Han, Lianchao, and Bradley A. Thayer, *Understanding the China Threat* (London: Routledge, 2023).

Hattendorf, John B., *The Evolution of the U.S. Navy's Maritime Strategy*, Newport Papers No. 20 (2004). Available at: digital-commons.usnwc.edu /usnwc-newport-papers/20

Ismay, Lord, *The Memoirs of General Lord Ismay* (New York: Viking Press, 1960).

Keller, Bill, "Gorbachev Visits Beijing for Start of Summit Talks," *New York Times*, May 15, 1989. Available at: nytimes.com/1989/05/15/world /gorbachev-visits-beijing-for-start-of-summit-talks.html

Koht, John, "Yang Reportedly Says Carrier to Be Purchased," *South China Morning Post*, 14 December 1992, p.10.

Krepinevich, Andrew F., and Barry D. Watts, *The Last Warrior: Andrew Marshall and the Shaping of Modern American Defense Strategy* (New York: Basic Books, 2015).

Kristof, Nicholas, "Deng Is Silent, and the Chinese Can't Tell Where the Power Is," *New York Times*, September 17, 1989. Available at: www .nytimes.com/1989/09/17/weekinreview/the-world-deng-is-silent-and -the-chinese-can-t-tell-where-the-power-is.html

Kristof, Nicholas, "Hu Yaobang, Ex-Party Chief in China, Dies at 73," *New*

York Times, April 16, 1989. Available at: www.nytimes.com/1989/04/16/obituaries/hu-yaobang-ex-party-chief-in-china-dies-at-73.html

Lague, David, "U.S. Commander Given Tour by Chinese Military," *New York Times*, August 21, 2007. Available at: www.nytimes.com/2007/08/21/world/asia/21cnd-china.html

Layton, RADM Edwin T., USN (Ret.), *And I Was There: Pearl Harbor and Midway Breaking the Secrets* (New York: William Morrow, 1985).

Lilley, James, with Jeffrey Lilley, *China Hands: Nine Decades of Adventure, Espionage, and Diplomacy in Asia* (New York: PublicAffairs, 2004).

Lowther, William, "U.S.' Blair defends 'turd' comment, Taiwan record," *Taipei Times*, February 19, 2000. Available at: taipeitimes.com/News/taiwan/archives/2009/02/01/2003434953

Mahadzir, Dzirhan, "VIDEO: China Coast Guard Blast Philippine Military Resupply with Water Cannons," *USNI News*, August 7, 2023. Available at: news.usni.org/2023/08/07/video-china-coast-guard-blast-philippine-military-resupply-with-water-canons

Mann, James, *About Face: A History of America's Curious Relationship with China, from Nixon to Clinton* (New York: Knopf, 1999).

Mann, James, *The China Fantasy: Why Capitalism Will Not Bring Democracy to China* (New York: Penguin, 2007).

Mann, James, "U.S.-China Relationship: Economics and Security in Perspective," written testimony before the U.S.-China Economic and Security Review Commission hearing, February 1, 2007. Available at: uscc.gov/sites/default/files/2.1.2007mann_james_statement.pdf

Martinson, Ryan D., *Echelon Defense: The Role of Sea Power in Chinese Maritime Dispute Strategy*, US Naval War College, China Maritime Studies Institute Red Books, Study No. 15, (2018). Available at: digital-commons.usnwc.edu/cgi/viewcontent.cgi?article=1014&context=cmsi-red-books

Medlicott, W. N. and Dorothy K. Coveney, eds., *Bismarck and Europe* (London: Edward Arnold, 1971).

"Military Must Focus on Current Wars, Gates Says," *NBC News/Associated Press*, May 13, 2008. Available at: nbcnews.com/id/wbna2460021

Mintz, John, "Missile Failures Led to Loral-China Link," *Washington Post*,

June 12, 1998. Available at: www.washingtonpost.com/wp-srv/politics /special/campfin/stories/rocket061298.htm

Mutual Defense Treaty between the Republic of the Philippines and the United States of America. Signed in Washington, D.C., August 30, 1951. Available at: www.officialgazette.gov.ph/1951/08/30/mutual-defense-treaty-between -the-republic-of-the-philippines-and-the-united-states-of-america-august -30–1951

Nakamura, Ryo, "US and Philippines Rapidly Draw Near to Counter China," *Nikkei*, May 2, 2023. Available at: asia.nikkei.com/Politics/International -relations/U.S.-and-Philippines-rapidly-draw-near-to-counter-China

National Counterintelligence and Security Center, "Safeguarding Our Future: US Business Risk: People's Republic of China (PRC) Laws Expands Beijing's Oversight of Foreign and Domestic Companies," June 20, 2023. Available at: www.dni.gov/files/NCSC/documents/SafeguardingOurFuture/FINAL _NCSC_SOF_Bulletin_PRC_Laws.pdf

Naughton, Barry, "The Impact of the Tiananmen Crisis on China's Economic Transition," in Jean-Philippe Béja, ed., *The Impact of China's 1989 Tiananmen Massacre* (London: Routledge, 2011), pp. 154–178.

New York Times, "Chinese Invited to Watch U.S. Exercises off Guam," May 15, 2006. Available at: www.nytimes.com/2006/05/15/world/asia/15thiht -games.htl. Accessed: September 12, 2023.

Nye, Joseph S., Jr., *Bound to Lead: The Changing Nature of American Power* (New York: Basic Books, 1991).

Nye, Joseph S., Jr., *Soft Power: The Means to Success in World Politics* (New York: Public Affairs, 2005).

Obama, President Barack, "Remarks by the President at Cairo University, 6–04-09," Cairo University, June 4, 2009. Available at: obamawhitehouse. archives.gov/the-press-office/remarks-president-cairo-university-6–04-09

Obama, President Barack, "Remarks by President Obama to the Australia Parliament," Canberra, Australia, November 17, 2011. Available at: obamawhitehouse.archives.gov/the-press-office/2011/11/17/remarks-president -obama-australian-parliament

O'Keeffe, Kate, and Aruna Viswanatha, "A DuPont China Deal Reveals Cracks in US National-Security Screening," *Wall Street Journal*, August

12, 2023. Available at: www.wsj.com/articles/a-dupont-china-deal-reveals
-cracks-in-u-s-national-security-screening-665cb50c?st=23ezcvp2w
b3l57r&reflink=article_email_share

Owens, Bill, "America Must Start Treating China as a Friend," *Financial Times*, November 17, 2009. Available at: ft.com/content/69241506-d3b2
–11de-8caf-00144feabdc0

Paterson, Stewart, *China, Trade and Power: Why the West's Economic Engagement Has Failed* (Padstow: London Publishing Partnership, 2018).

Perlez, Jane, and Grace Tatter, "Shared Secrets: How the U.S. and China Worked Together to Spy on the Soviet Union," WBUR "The Great Wager" Podcast, February 18, 2022. Available at: www.wbur.org/hereand now/2022/02/18/great-wager-spy-soviet-union

Pessin, Al, "US Commander Calls Chinese Interest in Aircraft Carriers 'Understandable,'" Voice of America, May 12, 2007. Available at: www .voanews.com/a/a-13-2007-05-12-voa5/332480.html. Accessed: September 12, 2023.

Peterson, Jonathan, "Clinton Was Warned Against China Launch," *Los Angeles Times*, May 23, 1998. Available at: www.latimes.com/archives /la-xpm-1998-may-23-mn-52739-story.html

Pillsbury, Michael, *The Hundred-Year Marathon: China's Secret Strategy to Replace America as the Global Superpower* (New York: Henry Holt, 2015).

Pompeo, United States Secretary of State Michael R., "Communist China and the Free World's Future," Remarks at the Richard Nixon Presidential Library and Museum, July 23, 2020. Available at: sv.usembassy.gov /secretary-michael-r-pompeo-remarks-at-the-richard-nixon-presidential -library-and-museum-communist-china-and-the-free-worlds-future

Powell, Robert, *In the Shadow of Power: States and Strategies in International Politics* (Princeton, N.J.: Princeton University Press, 1999).

Raimondo, Gina, "US Secretary of Commerce Gina Raimondo Delivers Remarks Ahead of Bilateral Meeting with PRC Minister of Commerce Wang Wentao," US Commerce Department, 28 August 2023, Available at: www.commerce.gov/news/speeches/2023/08/us-secretary-commerce-gina -raimondo-delivers-remarks-ahead-bilateral-meeting

Richard, Charles, former Commander, US Strategic Command, "Virtual

Event: A Conversation with Admiral Richard," Hudson Institute, August 26, 2021. Available at: s3.amazonaws.com/media.hudson.org /Transcript-%20A%20Conversation%20with%20Admiral%20Richard. pdf.

Schifrin, Nick, and Dan Sagalyn, "Indo-Pacific Commander Discusses Rising Tensions with China, Future of the Region," *PBS News Hour*, December 15, 2022. Available at: www.pbs.org/newshour/show /pacific-commander-of-u-s-navy-discusses-rising-tensions-with-china -future-of-region

"Stay the Course on China: An Open Letter to President Trump," *Journal of Political Risk*, July 18, 2019. Available at: www.jpolrisk.com/stay-the -course-on-china-an-open-letter-to-president-trump

Strassler, Robert B., ed., *The Landmark Thucydides: A Comprehensive Guide to the Peloponnesian War* (New York: Free Press, 1996).

Sutton, H. I., "North Korea's New Submarine Carries 10 Nuclear Missiles," *Naval News*, September 8, 2023. Available at: www.navalnews.com/naval -news/2023/09/north-koreas-new-submarine-carries-10-nuclear-missiles

Thayer, Bradley A., "Colin Gray and Strategic Thought," *Comparative Strategy*, Vol. 40, No. 2 (2021), pp. 128–132.

Thayer, Bradley A., "While the US Wasn't Watching, China Became the Strategic Beneficiary of 9/11," *The Hill*, March 8, 2019. Available at: thehill.com/opinion/international/431620-while-the-us-wasnt-watching -china-became-strategic-beneficiary-of-9-11

Thayer, Bradley A., and Lianchao Han, "Our Real Problem with China: Xi Jinping," *The Spectator*, May 10, 2019. Available at: spectator.us /problem-china-xi-jinping/

Timberlake, Edward, and William C. Triplett II, *Red Dragon Rising: Communist China's Military Threat to America* (Washington DC: Regnery Publishing, 1998).

Triplett, William C., II, "Dangerous Embrace," *New York Times*, September 10, 1994, Available at: www.nytimes.com/1994/09/10/opinion/danger- ous-embrace.html?searchResultPosition=167.

Tyler, Patrick, *A Great Wall: Six Presidents and China an Investigative History* (New York: Century Foundation, 1999).

United Kingdom, The National Archives, CAB 23/15/616A, dated August 15, 1919, p. 1. Available at: filestore.nationalarchives.gov.uk/pdfs/small/cab-23–15-wc-616a.pdf

US Department of Defense, *Quadrennial Defense Review Report* (Washington, D.C.: Department of Defense, 2006).

United States Statutes at Large, 1939–41, Vol. 54, Part 1 (Washington, D.C.: Government Printing Office, 1941). Available at: www.history.navy.mil /browse-by-topic/wars-conflicts-and-operations/world-war-ii/1941 /prelude/naval-expansion-act-14-june-1940.html

von Clausewitz, Carl, *On War*, edited and translated by Michael Howard and Peter Paret, (Princeton, N.J.: Princeton University Press, 1976).

Walt, Stephen M., *The Origins of Alliances* (Ithaca, N.Y.: Cornell University Press, 1987).

Waltz, Kenneth N., *Man, the State and War: A Theoretical Analysis* (New York: Columbia University Press, 1959).

Waltz, Kenneth N., "International Structure, National Force, and the Balance of World Power," in James N. Rosenau, ed., *International Politics and Foreign Policy* (New York: Free Press, 1969).

Waltz, Kenneth N., *Theory of International Politics* (Reading, Mass.: Addison-Wesley, 1979).

Waltz, Kenneth N., "The Emerging Structure of International Politics," *International Security*, Vol. 18, No. 2 (Fall 1993), pp. 44–79.

Wortzel, Larry M., "Missionary Zeal, Profits, and Constituent Interests," in Shiping Hua, ed., *The Political Logic of the U.S.-China Trade War* (Lanham, MD: Lexington Books, 2022), pp. 171–192.

Xinhua, "Ministry of Foreign Affairs: US Anti-China Open Letter Cannot Dictate the Direction of Sino-US Relations," (外交部：美反华公开信左右不了中美关系前进方向), July 22, 2019. Available at: www.xin-huanet.com/world/2019–07/22/c_1124784885.htm

Xu, Jian, "Rethinking China's Period of Strategic Opportunity," *China International Studies* (March/April 2014), pp. 51–70. Available at: www.ciis.org.cn/english/2014–05/28/content_6942258.htm

Zoellick, Robert B., "Whither China? From Membership to Responsibility," Remarks to National Committee on U.S.–China Relations, New York, NY, September 21, 2005.

INDEX